ECONOMICS FOR A ROUND EARTH

ECONOMICS
FOR A
ROUND EARTH

Charles A. Pierce

VANTAGE PRESS
New York / Los Angeles / Chicago

Contents

Foreword

When dealing with economics, we are confronted by a large array of interdependent static and dynamic variables. A change in one effects changes in all, which in turn affect the variable first changed through its interdependence with the rest.

Cybernetics is perhaps most appropriate for the treatment of economic matters. An economic system, being the means whereby an advanced living organism maintains its life and develops itself, can be looked upon as an analog of a living organism. It is in the whole greater than the sum of its parts. It has a life of its own. It can suffer good or bad health, age, be rejuvenated, and evolve over time. It consumes and excretes, has strengths and limitations. It can adapt to some extent to circumstances, and conversely can up to a point adapt its environment to its demands.

In the following examination of the modern world economy, it will occur that the same topic is treated, or the same statement made, several times.

It is difficult to deal with economics by chopping it up into neat chapters that can be dealt with in sequence. The subject must be dealt with in pieces but with the entirety always in view.

Looking at it from many different angles brings the same components repeatedly into view in different contexts. The repetitive introduction of particular concepts or the restating of certain points becomes necessary when exploring the dynamic system by different routes, which reveal new sets of interrelationships and consequences in which the statements and concepts previously set forth play some part.

Many subjects will be mentioned in the course of a particular discussion, with a promise to discuss them in a later chapter or a reference to a previous chapter. This is better than constantly breaking up a flow of thought with digressions and digressions within digressions.

ECONOMICS FOR A ROUND EARTH

Ends and Means

Good Trends, Not Good Conditions

It is not the intention in this book to establish a perfect world of perfect conditions. Such a thing has been imagined and described by many in the past, but it must always remain an abstract possibility in the indefinite future. What we should be doing is not seeking to establish a perfect world where there is no more need to progress; to cease to progress is to be dead. Rather we should seek to establish positive trends; an improvement here, there, going on all the time.

In judging the state of a nation, we should not look just at the actual conditions at any time, but at the trends. Is that country getting better? If so, how fast?

It may be that a nation with fully developed civil rights and democratic institutions, which however are deteriorating through neglect and abuse, being ignored by complacent citizens and manipulated by cynical politicians, is worse off than a nation oppressed by totalitarian violence and superstition where, however, democratic ideas are spreading and democratic institutions are forming in embryo.

It is on trends that the people judge a government at election time. The actual level of unemployment, for example, is no indicator of the likely outcome of an election; the rate and direction of change of unemployment level is the indicator. A high level of unemployment on the way down will help the government return; a much lower level of unemployment on the way up may give the reins to the opposition.

In dealing with economics, a subject of great importance in humanity's relationship with the life-supporting environment of this planet, I only seek to set in train progressive trends, to break away from a static attachment to economic notions that have remained basically the same for thousands of years notwithstanding clever superstructures of ideas which have been built upon them in the last couple of centuries. I do not promise a perfect world economy or know when that may be achieved or precisely what its form may be; but I hope for a better world economy, that is, a more sustainable, more life-oriented economy, and one that will continue to improve in those directions. The goal is to provide a stable context in which humanity can be, not perfect, but able to continue its muddled and harrowing progress towards perfection.

Evolution, Not Revolution

Achieving this sustainable world economy would be nothing less than a great step in human evolution, comparable with the mastery of fire or the development of settled agriculture as opposed to hunting and gathering. It concerns the whole world and needs to be tackled on a world, not just a national, basis. This does not mean that people within nations can do nothing; it means that what they do, they do not for Australia, or for America, but for the world in their own countries, not as Australians or Americans but as *Weltbuerger.*

Also, the evolutionary step is a vast change from our present world setup.

Faced with this enormous gap between here and there, it is difficult for people to get involved, develop a coherent plan, or keep going. It is not just a matter, as some lesser

2

issues may be, of boiling around for a few years, changing a government by votes or violence, and having the appropriate measures legislated and implemented in a generation or so.

The method must be evolution, not revolution. Nations and individuals are constantly confronted by myriad choices, big and small, in all areas. To choose one option is consistent with moving towards a stable and ecologically sound relationship between humanity and the world; choosing the other pushes against it. By constantly making the choices in the appropriate direction, the human world can evolve steadily in the right way. There will be a lot of damage and loss en route due not to the choices that are being made, but to the fact that the evolutionary process that they comprise is too slow to prevent bad effects from destructive interaction with our environment. But there's no other way. By this means, organisations and governments can have something to do, and comprehend, and care about all the time.

Examples follow of events that can develop in two directions, one of which contributes to progress towards a sustainable world economy, while the other retards such progress.

Some of the examples may puzzle or disconcert, but the rest of the book is supposed to explain the thinking behind them.

A government should stay in rather than leave, or join rather than stay out of, a supranational body such as the European Common Market.

Tariff barriers should be lowered rather than raised, or removed rather than erected. This helps transfer throughput (economic activity, consumption, and so on; the term is explained more fully later) from more to less perfluent nations.

The words *perfluent* and *perfluence* are preferable to *affluent* and *affluence* because they describe wealth flowing through rather than flowing to. This will be discussed later.

3

The creation of cartels and subsequent increases in the price of resources such as oil is a helpful event because it slows the depletion rate of resources and again helps transfer throughput from higher to lower perfluence areas.

People should decide to use a push-bike or public transport instead of their car even a little more often or merely get a smaller car. Larger changes are more useful, but small changes also contribute if they are the best a person can manage.

A strike called in any industry is useful because it stops throughput through that industry and buys time for the whole system to change to a sustainable one. Every bit of time bought is useful because the time needed is long. The loss of pay by workers on strike also retards throughput.

If an electorate chooses a government whose policies are incompetent and result in a lower throughput rate (or gross national "product") this is usually regarded as a bad thing, but it is good for moving towards the sustainable economy because it slows resource depletion, buys time, and makes the inept government's country more dependent on other parts of the human family.

Industries that feed on endangered species, such as whaling and seal-hunting, should be limited or closed. They will limit or close themselves anyway through their continued activity, but then the endangered species would no longer exist at the end. So the commonsense measure is to limit the industries while the species on which they depend can still recover.

If two or more nations unite even in a small way, this is useful. Small steps towards unity, achieving progress without making anyone feel threatened, include eliminating passports and work permits between countries; uniting customs and excise; using a common currency as legal tender in any of the countries; putting separate armed forces under a unified supranational command; adopting a single head of state for all countries involved; merging into supranational bodies government departments administering areas that naturally transcend national borders, such as environment, the seas and inland waters, air pollution, long-distance transport; co-operating on projects too big for one country to handle effectively, such as fusion or solar energy or space exploration.

Similarities of language and political systems would ease the merging of separate nations. Possible likely mergers might be Argentina with Chile, the two Germanys and Austria (despite the unfortunate precedent in that case), Australia and New Zealand, the United States of America and Canada, Central American countries. The current pressure for fragmentation of countries into smaller autonomous units based on religion or race or language runs against the requirement of a sustainable world economy, which is for world political unity prevailing in harmony with ethnic diversity. The pressure for political fragmentation is a response to, but not a cure for, the pressures of increasing human population against limited and depleting world resources.

Migration of people from heavily populated to less populated parts of the world is a helpful trend. It is resisted more or less fiercely, but is likely to continue and must be accommodated to. Each small step in the process is helpful; for example, one Asian helped to arrive and settle in Australia is a contribution.

The issue of nuclear arms control is difficult. The economic activity diverted into immobile stores of potential mass death should be turned to more life-loving uses. But in practice, under present conditions the released economic activity would accelerate the resource depletion that is threatening the human economy and much other life. Also, a complete absence of nuclear weapons would remove what has been for forty years a decisive obstacle to repeated global wars on a scale much greater than the first two. These wars, with all the power of modern technology except nuclear fission, could

5

well be just as destructive to life and to the earth's life-supporting capacity as the dreaded all-out nuclear holocaust, though taking longer about it and leaving no radioactive fission products. Vietnam was a microcosm of what we might expect.

It would be better if total, general nuclear disarmament were not campaigned for directly as such, but, rather, made to come about by redirecting all the campaigners' caring and energy into working away at the other issues and thereby gradually creating a world where nuclear weapons will "wither on the vine" as redundant, irrelevant relics of a less advanced humanity. The real peril is not the nuclear weapons as such, but conflicts and instabilities that provoke their construction and would ignite endless wars in their absence.

Saving a single swamp from becoming a rubbish tip or car-park, or a single tree from being felled, or a few kilometres of road from being laid through an ecologically sensitive or aesthetically pleasing area, or just buying and throwing out less "rubbish," are local, manageable issues which all contribute.

So, the program of activity for ordinary people is to latch onto any issue in which they feel interested or expert and do what they can to influence the resolution of an issue in the appropriate direction. That accomplished, another issue can be tackled. The issue can be one having no obvious connection with what the public thinks of as being ecological or environmental, but its resolution in the appropriate direction will contribute to the achievement of an ecologically stable world and a sustainable human economy.

Notes on Evolution, Not Revolution

First, it will be noted that things that common sense tells us are always good, such as efficient government or nuclear disarmament, or always bad, such as strikes or cartels, may actually be bad sometimes and good other times depending on the circumstances.

Second, because a thing is evil, it doesn't have to be removed; its presence may obstruct a greater evil. It may be the symptom of evil causes; there is no point in fighting the symptom while neglecting its causes. And campaigning directly against an evil may not be the best way of getting rid of it.

Third, the gross differences in perfluence (level of consumption of goods and services) between different parts of the world human population must be levelled out by any and every means. This doesn't necessarily mean that there should be no rich or poor individuals, but that differences in perfluence that are unjust or, what is more important, perceived to be unjust between different parts of the world are a source of instability and conflict and a barrier to the development of a sustainable world economy.

Fourth, world political and economic unity is necessary and must be worked towards, but need not be inconsistent with ethnic and cultural diversity.

Fifth, it might seem that if all economic activity were to stop, we would have a sustainable economy. This is true, but not the aim here. The task before us is to enable the human species to thrive indefinitely, supported by an economic system that is complex and lively but yet still sustainable.

The task may be compared to changing a complex mosaic design on a huge wall for a different, more complex mosaic. Faced with the totality of the task, anyone would be daunted and lapse into apathy. But if you say to one person or group, "Do what you can to change these ten stones here consistent with the overall design" and to another, "Do what you can to change these twenty stones here consistent with the overall design," then the job looks manageable to everyone and can steadily be accomplished as the result of many small efforts.

7

Concepts and Terms

The world economy isn't working as well as it should and could. Some countries that enjoyed for some years near full employment, low interest rates, and a bearable rate of price increases, with fast-rising material living standards, all achieved without anything like current high levels of government and private debt, do so no longer. Efforts to restore those happy conditions have had no durable success.

Perhaps current economics of whatever school, from the left to the right, confuses quantities with their rates of change, describes phenomena in terms opposite to their nature, misrepresents things in harmony as being contradictory and vice versa.

Wealth is currently understood to be money, goods, and services.

In fact, wealth is environmental resources—clean air and water; metal ores; biological diversity, that is the number and variety of living organisms; fossil fuels; timber; arable land; fish; natural recycling and cleansing systems; pleasant living and recreational environments; the earth's capacity as a home for life.

Goods and services are wealth in the process of throughput.

Money, people, technology, skill, manufacturing equipment are not resources or wealth. All are agents of throughput. Technology and skill being agents of throughput could be regarded as qualitative wealth, which is quite distinct from quantitative wealth, the feedstock of throughput.

Money facilitates throughput but the total money quantity isn't the important variable. What matters is the proportion of the total money supply flowing through the different channels in the economy—wages, profits, investment, government spending, transfer payments. This proportionate flow theory will be discussed more fully later, in various chapters.

"Production?"

Structuring, or realising, wealth into goods and services is called production or output, as though wealth were being created. Rather, this structuring or realisation is part of the process of throughput of wealth. The use of goods and services, now called consumption in the sense of being opposite to "production," is really a subsequent process in the throughput chain whereby wealth is degraded into waste matter and heat whence it may be renewed.

For example, fresh clean water is degraded into dirty water whence it can evaporate and fall again as clean rain, or else be filtered by natural or human processes to become clean water again. In both types of renewal the throughput of some other form of wealth is involved. The first requires solar radiation; the second needs clean earth or some other filter, healthy organisms, or chemicals.

As another example, the burning of fuel produces carbon dioxide that nourishes plants, which in turn can directly or indirectly become fuel again. In this case the renewal process involves the throughput of topsoil, nutrients, and fuel.

Renewal need not always be back to the original resource, i.e., wealth-form. It may be sufficient and even preferable to go back only as far as an earlier stage of the throughput chain. This applies to metals. Impure corroded metals from used up metal articles may be recycled back to a state of purer metal ready for restructuring into new articles. This renewal requires the throughput of fuel and other resources.

The Throughput Chain

The throughput chain comprises several "links," different processes that follow one another but do not all necessarily take place at the same rate. The processes commonly are: the extraction or controlling of wealth; its rendering or structuring into saleable goods and services; the sale of those goods and services; and their subsequent degradation into waste matter from which wealth may be renewed.

Crude oil provides one illustration of fluctuations in the relative rates of the throughput "links." Sometimes oil is being pumped out of the ground faster than it is being refined into a range of fuels and chemicals, sometimes more slowly. Sometimes the refinement process is faster than the sale and consumption processes. At other times refinement lags behind sale and consumption, or sale may be faster than consumption, or vice versa.

The relation between the various rates is an important determinant of prices. This relation is thus a determinant of the rates of sale and consumption. Changes in these affect the rates of the previous links in the throughput chain. This in turn affects again the rates of sale and consumption. A change in the rate of any of the links, which are all interdependent variables, does not just effect a simple alteration in the others. It is more in the nature of a disturbance which knocks the entire chain into an agitation that can settle into a new dynamic equilibrium.

Many people think that the "oil crisis" of the 1970s has been put behind us. In the 1970s there was supposed to be a world shortage of fossil oil; prices had to go up; we had to consume less, get smaller cars, get the bus, get on our bikes. In the mid-1980s we hear that OPEC are in trouble, "production" (i.e., extraction) of oil has to be cut to prop up prices, there is a glut of oil on the world market.

The reality is that there has been no sudden, dramatic turnabout in the world's fossil oil situation. Fossil oil is still a limited resource; its rate of consumption has risen in the last ten years; it is still being depleted by being consumed at a rate much faster than its renewal rate; it is still being consumed faster than could be permitted by any known renewable replacement resource (see chapter "Nonrenewable Resources—Leave Them in the Ground?") and it has been depleted considerably in the last ten years—in fact the oil situation today is worse than ten years ago, not better.

The illusion of a great improvement in oil supplies is created by changes in the relationships among different links in the throughput chain.

In the 1960s and 1970s, consumption of fossil oil was straining to get ahead of the rate of extraction and refinement of oil. This, combined with low prices and profligate consumption, made it easy for nations with large oil resources within their borders to gang together, restrict their extraction rates, and boost prices. This took place from 1973 onwards.

The reaction to this altered the relations in the throughput chain. Prices and taxes for oil products increased. Economies slowed their rate of increase in throughput (currently called their "economic growth" rate). People went for smaller cars or caught busses to work, and there was a boom in the use of bicycles. Oil for heating was replaced to a great extent by better insulation, solar heating, gas, electricity; oil previously burnt to generate electricity was replaced more and more by coal, nuclear fission, natural gas, hydroelectricity, geothermals, and so on.

While this was going on, countries with oil reserves untapped or not being extracted as fast as they possibly could be borrowed huge sums of money to extract oil faster, build more refining capacity, and pay for all sorts of things that

11

they wanted to have now in the expectation that oil revenues would pay off the debt in the future (see also chapter "Borrowing to Invest to Get Rich").

The result of all this has been that oil can currently be extracted and refined at a considerably faster rate than that at which the market is able to consume it. So the first link in the throughput chain, extraction, is too big for the subsequent consumption link—quite the reverse of the situation in the 1960s and 1970s described earlier. Extraction and refinement are put under stress by a rate of consumption lower than they could allow. This does not change the facts of the world's oil situation, but it changes the direction of the pressure on the prices of oil and oil products—downward pressure now instead of upward pressure earlier. This change in the direction of pressure on prices is really the only change that has occurred, but it serves to create an illusion that the world oil supply situation itself has dramatically changed.

Conversely, a resource can be renewable, plentiful in supply, and being consumed at a rate comfortably below its renewal rate. But mismatching between the links in the throughput chain of this resource can create the illusion of shortage by putting upward pressure on prices.

To sum up, the throughput of resources takes place through several stages. Mismatches in the potential rates of these different stages have large effects on the price of the resource and of goods made from it. But these effects are artefacts of human behaviour and market forces and may have little to do with the depletion rate, renewal rate, quantity of the resource, or how much danger to the economy is threatened by its rate of consumption at the time.

The continued excessive and unnecessary consumption of oil poses, if anything, a greater economic threat today than ten years ago despite the current benign price environment. Once oil-producing countries have either paid off or defaulted

12

on their debts and abandoned enough industrial plant and grand economic schemes to adjust to a lower rate of extraction, then, since world oil consumption continues to rise, another "price shock" can be expected later with analogous consequences to those already experienced. It would be better to take the matter in hand with deliberate policy measures aimed at minimising oil consumption, instead of just letting things happen. Such measures need not be reinvented here; what they ought to be has been widely understood and discussed elsewhere. The problem is not working out what the measures should be, but implementing them—a political problem.

The Throughput Chain and World Hunger

There is a sad anomaly when we consider today's world food situation. On one hand, hundreds of millions of people in less perfluent nations are demonstrably underfed; on the other, thousands of farmers in, for instance, the U.S.A. and Australia are going bankrupt, losing their farms, because their food crops are excess to effective demand (which means ability to pay rather than physical need) and fail to command a price sufficient to cover costs, service loans, and live at a material level acceptable in their society. Food continues to pile up in silos and caves.

So is the world short of food or not, in the sense that can enough food be realised to keep every person in the world adequately nourished?

Obviously if the world human population keeps increasing there will certainly come a time when insufficient food can be realised for every person. But there is evidence to suggest that if the world's population stopped growing now it would be possible, for a time anyway, to feed the present population adequately. Whether this level of food realisation

13

could be sustained without depleting resources (consuming resources faster than their renewal rate) is another question.

The starving millions—bankrupt farmers anomaly can be explained in terms of the throughput chain. There is a break in this chain between the abundance of food that could be realised by farmers in the more perfluent countries, and the abundance of stomachs elsewhere that don't get enough food. The break in the chain results from the farmers wanting too much payment for their food and the hungry having too little to pay for it. The hungry lack the command of goods and services that would enable them to satisfy the farmers' demands to an extent sufficient to get enough food.

This problem originates in the fact of the excessive differences in perfluence among the world's people. Many are paid too little for their work; a minority are paid too much. The "poorest" in countries like Australia and the U.S.A. take for granted a command of goods and services that most of the world's people regard as luxury beyond their reach.

Measures to move towards a more equitable distribution of the world's throughput can gradually feed the hungry better and improve the viability of those farming enterprises presently so financially troubled in the more perfluent nations. This is discussed further in the following digression.

Digression: Farmers and Miners in Trouble

Besides the bankrupt farmers—hungry people anomaly in the previous chapter, prices for many metals are depressed and mines are closing because although these metals are needed, they cannot be purchased at prices sufficient for the mining companies to remain viable.

These anomalies point up the difference between actual demand (the need for goods) and effective demand (the ability to pay for goods).

The heavy burden of debt-servicing on so many less perfluent countries deprives them of cash with which to feed their people and improve their material standard of living. (See a later chapter "Borrowing to Invest to Get Rich".) The huge debt burden has reduced effective demand, world-wide. All the heavy borrowing has aggravated poverty, not reduced it.

During the Great Depression of the 1930s there was within nations a similar anomaly. Goods, or the labor and plant for structuring goods, existed side by side with the need for those goods without the cash being available to employ the labor, make the goods, and meet the need.

Policies were eventually developed on a national scale to inject the cash where it was needed and link labor, resources, and markets together to provide full employment and satisfied needs.

Analogous policies are required today on an international scale to link the hungry of some nations with the desperate farmers of others.

This should not be done by heavily indebted countries defaulting on loans. This would set a terrible precedent that debtor governments, companies, and individuals everywhere would be clamouring to follow and the world economy would be damaged so much that the poor would be worse off, not better. (Of course the world ecosystem would benefit from the resulting sharp drop in resource throughput, but the aim of this book is to point to ways in which a healthy ecosystem and a useful developing human economy can exist indefinitely in harmony with each other.)

It would be better to find a way that would achieve the same result by a different channel, a way that would conform to accepted precedents in kind, if not in degree, and that wouldn't itself set dangerous or uncontrollable precedents.

Heavily indebted nations could be given large sums of money as a gift, not to pay off all their loans, but to reduce the debt enough to reduce payments servicing the debt to an extent that would give the debtors a better chance of repaying the rest while having more of their national throughput diverted from the sterile servicing of debt to the purchase of needed food and resources.

Where is this money to come from? Governments are usually responsible for foreign aid grants, but this is out of the question because the governments of the most perfluent nations are themselves deeply in debt.

The money should come from the private sectors of the most perfluent nations. A fund should be started, enough to clear off, say, 25 percent of the outstanding debts of a list of countries that would have to be decided according to a set of criteria but that would certainly include Brazil, Mexico, Argentina, and Poland. A campaign would have to be started to convince cash-rich companies and individuals everywhere that their contribution to this fund would be not a charitable write-off, but an investment in a healthier world economy that would benefit them in ways both direct and indirect, from bigger markets for their goods to lower interest rates and easier loans.

The Derivatives of Wealth

The terms *derivative* and *differential* are used here in their mathematical sense, denoting rates of change.

Gross national product and living standard are treated as measures of quantity of wealth. In fact, they are not the

16

quantity but its first derivative or first differential, the rate of wealth-throughput. The other first derivative is the rate of renewal of wealth. This rate varies from one resource to another.

If the rate of throughput is faster than the rate of renewal for every vital resource, as is the case in the world today, the world economy is in an unsustainable state. The throughput rate, the world level of economic activity, cannot continue indefinitely at its present level; still less can it go on increasing indefinitely.

The throughput rate must inevitably fall; how far or fast or in how many jerks it does so is not predictable with the same certainty. But however it happens, jobs will be destroyed and material living standards lowered.

Consider the resources for which the throughput rate is currently higher than the renewal rate: oil, gas, and coal; fissionable uranium; arable land; potable water; marine animal life; all major metal ores; forests; biological diversity; oxygen-producing oceanic phytoplankton. Others could be listed.

Economic growth is currently taken to mean the rate of increase of wealth. Actually it is the rate of increase of the rate of throughput of wealth. It is the second derivative of wealth. It could be called throughput increase, TI for short.

So what really is economic growth?

Economic Growth Redefined

A more accurate definition of economic growth would be any change in the relation between the throughput and renewal rates, for a given resource for which throughput exceeds renewal, in which change the ratio of the throughput rate to

17

the renewal rate falls, or conversely the ratio of renewal to throughput increases.

Thus economic growth, if redefined as proposed here, can be achieved by three means:

(i) Increasing the wealth base by reafforestation, farm land restoration, saving endangered species from extinction, to give a few examples. Note that discovering more oil, for instance, doesn't increase the wealth base. The oil was not brought into existence by discovery; it was already there, already part of the wealth base. Discovery only added it to the human-made list of "known reserves."

(ii) Economic growth is achievable by reducing the throughput rate, if throughput exceeds renewal for a particular resource. Examples are: restricting fishing or other cropping to allow stocks to build up; changing farming methods to reduce degradation and erosion loss of topsoil; cutting (by rationing or taxing) the consumption of fresh water, motor fuel, and other goods whose rate of use in many countries is far in excess of what is needed to achieve the purpose of the consumption. For example, if you only want to move one person a few kilometres you don't need a tonne or more of powerful machinery to do it, nor do you need to water large stretches of road for several hours a day just to keep a small piece of lawn green.

Other examples are:

Reducing, again possibly by tax and price manipulation, the acidification of fresh water bodies by vehicle fumes and industrial fuel burning;

Reducing the waste and pollution of often scarce and important habitats on the fringes of cities caused by using them to dump excessive quantities of "rubbish," much of which needn't be discarded or needn't even be manufactured and purchased in the first place.

In the former case the "throughput" of the lakes

18

and rivers is reduced by preventing their pollution with acid emissions and, in the latter, the throughput of wetlands and natural areas near cities is reduced.

(iii) If the throughput rate of a resource exceeds its renewal rate, then its renewal rate can be increased. This can be done by adding human renewal systems to natural ones or by increasing existing human ones. For instance metals, for whose ores the natural renewal rate is very low, can be recycled instead of piling up in dumps. There is no reason why most of the metal consumed today cannot repeatedly be recovered and reused. There are technical difficulties due to corrosion and mixture with other metals and non-metals, but there is no reason why these cannot be surmounted.

The issue of recycling being often "uneconomic" according to present economic concepts will be discussed in a later chapter ("Digression: Renewal and Recycling of Resources; Wages and Jobs").

It might seem that points two and three, reducing throughput and increasing renewal, are the same thing as point one, increasing the wealth base; or that points two and three amount to the same thing. It is true that the three points are interrelated but it is necessary to draw a distinction between on the one hand physically increasing the quantity of a resource, and on the other changing the rates of use and of regeneration of a resource. In point one we are dealing with the quantity, in two and three with its differentials.

So we arrive at a definition of economic growth quite different from the current one, which means increasing the throughput rate of as many resources as possible without regard to their quantities or renewal rates. The proposed new meaning would be, increasing the quantity of wealth or lowering its rate of depletion, often by reducing the throughput rate.

Many countries have believed themselves to be enjoying

economic growth for years and to be getting ever richer. But in resource terms they have been undergoing economic depletion and getting poorer.

To return to a qualifier added to the original definition of economic growth above, any change in the relationship between the throughput and renewal rates for a given resource for which throughput exceeds renewal, in which change the ratio of throughput to renewal falls or that of renewal to throughput rises, is economic growth.

The point here is that if the throughput rate for a resource is less than its available potential renewal rate, then any increase in the throughput rate up to the renewal rate should not affect the overall quantity of the resource. It is only when the throughput rate exceeds the available renewal rate that change in the relation between the two rates affects the quantity of the resource or wealth species.

Misconceptions in Practice

The inadequate or wrong concepts of current economics lead to a number of misconceptions, some examples of which will be given.

"Soak the Rich"

The "soak the rich" taxation policy advocated or practiced by the political left is based on a confusion about the nature of wealth.

The idea is to tax "wealth" from the "rich" members of society and redistribute it, making the rest of the people "richer."

20

But what the "rich" have is a disproportionate share, not of the country's wealth, a static variable, but rather of its throughput, a dynamic variable. One determinant of throughput is the incentive offered to the "movers and shakers" among business people to exercise their skills to the best advantage, to maximise throughput within the prevailing limits. This incentive lies in the extent to which they can increase and maintain their personal throughput. Taxing most of it away, nationalising businesses reduces the incentive and the national throughput rate.

The result is that the government has less throughput to redistribute than planned. So expectations must be disappointed, or, if they are to be met, this can only be in the short term at a greater cost of future throughput by borrowing from the future in the form of increased government budget deficits.

The consequences are that inflation takes place, due to the fall in throughput relative to the money supply, and heavy government borrowing and higher inflation exert upward pressure on interest rates.

These results reduce the throughput rate further, increasing the gap between expectations and what's achievable.

Private and government measures to close this gap will strengthen the forces that created the gap and thus be absolutely counterproductive if they take the form usual in recent years of more private and public borrowing, more insistent wage demands, more strikes, and further increases in the money supply.

This subject will recur in various contexts.

Global Inequalities in Wealth

Another misconception held by many in both "rich" and "poor" countries is that the "rich" should go on making and using ever more goods and services, thereby "creating wealth" that can somehow find its way to the "poor" nations making them "richer."

The true picture is quite different.

Some nations, the so-called rich, actually have much higher throughput than others. We can call these nations the more perfluent. The word "rich" denotes possession of wealth while "affluent" denotes wealth flowing to. Perfluent denotes wealth flowing through, which is the point here.

If these more perfluent economies keep boosting their throughput, using wealth not only from within their own borders but from all over the world, then the throughput available to less perfluent nations is subject to restriction and reduction. Not only do these nations become no more perfluent as a result of the increasing perfluence of the others, they become less so.

In terms of actual wealth, many less perfluent nations, because of great resources contained within their borders, are wealthier than many of the more perfluent ones.

Transfer of wealth between rich and poor nations, called for by the less perfluent, is already taking place with great vigour, but in the opposite direction to that intended by the advocates of the transfer.

The resources wealth of the less perfluent nations is being transferred to feed the greater throughput stream of the more perfluent. Too much wealth is going to the latter in exchange for too little throughput.

An analogy may be drawn between the world today and, for example, Britain in the eighteenth century.

At that place and time, a fraction of the population commanded most of the throughput. They claimed a right to do so by birth and station, a right that was taken for granted by them and conceded by most of the rest of the people.

If members of the perfluent class had a change in circumstances that caused them to have to make do with one servant, a small mansion, and only their legs to get about with, they thought of themselves as suffering hardship, even though their situation was vastly better than members of the majority could hope to achieve.

Today, a person in the more perfluent ("developed") nations is categorised by their government as living below the poverty line if they earn less than a certain amount per annum, even though this might enable them to enjoy a level of consumption of goods and services far above what the majority of the world's people can hope to aspire to. Far from being impoverished or deprived, the "poverty-line" dwellers in the most perfluent nations are members of the world's aristocracy, the privileged class.

If disparities in material living standard among the world's people can be reduced, this must be done by transferring throughput while slowing the transfer of actual wealth.

Rises in material living standards in more perfluent nations are in competition with such rises in the less perfluent, in the sense that both involve accelerated depletion of the world's limited store of wealth. It is true that throughput in some places stimulates throughput in others, through the mechanism of trade and investment. Thus rises in throughput in more perfluent places would, in a hypothetical unlimited world, always be able to raise throughput in others, however far behind. This is one assumption on which economic policies the world over are currently based. It is assumed that people in more perfluent areas should go on consuming more and more and thus eventually drag even the least perfluent of the world's people up to their level.

However, we do not live in an unlimited world but in a real, limited one, and material living standards must stabilise and, under present conditions, fall in more perfluent regions in order to give less perfluent countries a better chance of improving living standards. There's no other way. Rapidly increasing consumption of oil over decades in the more per-fluent world led to depletion of this non-renewable resource, thence to increases in oil prices that meant that less perfluent people had less access to oil. Not only does this directly reduce the availability of fuel, but in some places valuable agricultural land has been taken over for growing crops specifically for the purpose of providing alcohol fuel for motor vehicles. Overfishing to feed overconsumption in the more perfluent countries depletes the ocean's fish resource, whose renewal rate depends, inter alia, on the size of stocks and makes this food scarcer and more expensive for others. Other examples could be found.

People in less perfluent countries work harder in exchange for less spending power, that is command of goods and services, than those in more perfluent places. This is not due to any intrinsic inferiority of some people to others, but rather to historical legacies and artificial circumstances that are probably unjust and certainly changeable.

Money flowing from one nation to another can transfer throughput under these conditions:

If more money is demanded in exchange for the same unit of wealth. This happened with oil from 1973 onwards. It must happen with all other forms of wealth. Money represents throughput here, but of course the amount of throughput a unit of money represents falls over time. It is necessary for the money price rises to stay ahead of the rate of decrease in money value.

If the money is a straight-out gift, or a loan that becomes a gift through default.

Many countries in recent years have come dangerously close to defaulting on huge loans from international banks. The loans were initially arranged as a result of mistaken thinking by the borrowing governments.

Borrowing to Invest to Get Rich

Governments in many less perfluent nations have borrowed thousands of millions of dollars in recent years in attempting to achieve permanent increases in the level of national economic activity and living standards.

The belief was that by borrowing "wealth" from the "rich" nations, they would be able to use it to generate more "wealth" of their own, enough to pay back the original "wealth" with interest and still leave enough to make their own country permanently wealthier.

This sort of gambit can appear to work but also fail disastrously. Its chances of success can be greatly improved if the real nature of the transactions is understood.

Money represents throughput, and diversions of cash represent diversions of throughput. What the governments were borrowing was not wealth but throughput.

In return they were obliged to pay back not just the equivalent of the original throughput (less or more, depending on the change in value of the currency in which the loan was negotiated) but the equivalent of much more besides, the amount depending on the interest rate, the time over which the loan was to be repaid, and the self-reinforcing degree to which the repayments fell into arrears. A loan repayable at current high interest rates over many years can demand the return of many times the original amount of money.

So the original loan, in its net effect, is not a helpful transfer of a quantity of throughput from a more to a less perfluent nation, but a transfer of many times that amount in the reverse direction—quite the opposite of what's needed in today's world.

The borrowed throughput would have to generate many times itself, and then some. But wealth is what generates throughput, when acted on by throughput agents. Throughput is only a throughput agent to the extent that it consists of capital goods, i.e., manufacturing equipment that still needs wealth to feed it and to be throughput as goods and services. But wealth is not what has been borrowed, and a country's quantity of wealth is not increased at all by the money loan.

The other side of the coin is that the international banks who sold these huge loans, believing that huge profits (throughput gains) would thereby come their way, will gain far less than expected, if anything. This has caused and will cause great problems of solvency for them.

What should these present-day deeply indebted nations have done to improve their lot, rather than borrow huge amounts of money from international banks?

Useful measures have been suggested in an earlier chapter. Keeping always in mind that their aim is the direct transfer of throughput in their favour, less perfluent but wealthy nations should:

Follow the example of OPEC and raise the price, while restricting the supply of any resource that they export. The degree of success will vary, but the experience of OPEC shows that considerable success is possible with an important resource, even if the success only lasts a dozen years at a time.

Encourage tourism from high-perfluence countries and extract from tourists the maximum amount of hard currency while tolerating no large or permanent environmental interference from them.

Accept money as outright gifts, never as loans.

Fight by every means to tear down import barriers of whatever kind. More perfluent nations prop up high wages in many of their industries by restricting or discouraging the import of goods from similar industries in less perfluent places where wages, therefore prices, are lower. An absence of tariff barriers would force industries in more perfluent economies to cut wages or close down, in either case benefitting the less perfluent.

Environment "versus" Economic Progress

The fierce conflicts between conservationists on one side and workers, industrialists, and some poliicians on the other arise from a misconception on the part of the latter group.

Both parties in fact desire the same goal—economic well-being. But the latter and many of the former believe that environmental conservation and economic progress are conflicting aims, between which a balance or compromise must be found.

One party believes that the balance must be weighted heavily in favour of what they believe to be economic growth and development; the other holds that it must swing more towards environmental conservation.

The reality is that environmental conservation and enhancement and economic progress are complementary, not conflicting, goals. The environment is the fount of all resources whose throughput is economic activity. Failure to conserve the environment results in depletion of resources with consequent reduction of economic activity both in quality and quantity with loss of jobs and falling living standards.

The discussion of how economic activity is reduced will continue after the ensuing chapter.

Digression: "Pollution" Red Herrings

Litter "Pollution"

A misleading idea started when environmental awareness really took off world-wide in the late sixties and early seventies is that "pollution" means "litter" and that preventing litter means doing all that's necessary to prevent pollution and protect the environment. Many people still believe this.

This false idea was begun by the packaging industry in the U.S.A., which started a front organisation called the Keep America Beautiful Council. This has a faithful copy in Australia, founded by the same industry for the same reasons, called the Keep Australia Beautiful Council. The purpose of KABC was ostensibly to make everyone put litter in bins whence it could be carted off so as to keep the environment pretty. The real purpose was to keep sales of excess and disposable packaging high and rising. It was thought that if the amount of litter being chucked around went on increasing, public anger would force packaging reductions, recycling, and other measures that were seen by the packaging industry as a threat to their business.

In fact, the environmental pollution resulting from litter is not reduced by putting it all in bins whence it can be carted off to a concentrated area. Rather, pollution is increased because (i) concentrating the stuff in thick deposits makes it more difficult to degrade by natural processes, and (ii) the areas selected for dumping are of low value in real estate terms, but of relatively high ecological value compared to the urban areas whence the litter was collected.

These dumping areas are of low real estate value not because they are unpleasant, but because they are relatively far from urban facilities. They are of high ecological value because they are often swamps or wetlands, regarded as smelly or "unsightly" but essential seasonal or permanent habitats for myriad species of birds, amphibians, and insects. Other dumping areas are important reservoirs of diverse plant and mammal species.

For the best treatment of our natural environment, the answer is not to consume as much throwaway goods and packaging as we can and throw it all into the rubbish bins

28

provided. Rather the answer is first, to consume as little as possible and thus to throw away as little as possible. Second, what we do throw away should be spread about dead or near-dead areas, preferably roads and verges, carparks, paved areas, and vacant lots rather than green parkland. Wet rubbish such as garden cuttings and vegetable leavings should be used on suburban gardens as compost. Sewage and toxic chemicals cannot, of course, be disposed of in this way, but we should minimise the need to dispose of them at all.

Disposed of as suggested, the litter is easier to degrade by oxidation and sunlight and the areas on which it is preferably to be spread are not habitats for life that it can harm or restrict. Such spreading is ecologically neutral and does not deplete environmental resources, unlike the method of concentrated dumping in natural areas. In addition, the unpleasant appearance of the litter scattered about will create public pressure for reduced packaging generally and for more returnable containers.

This is another case where what is best ecologically goes directly against what is commonly thought of as good sense and correct behaviour. We must come to think of good sense and correct behaviour to be whatever best serves the purpose of conserving and enhancing the earth's life and life-supporting capacity, and let this goal override all the rest, ideas of tidiness and propping up particular industries.

Why do the packaging industries go to the length of creating bogus "environmental" organisations to try to maintain and increase their sales? Not because they are evil or fascist or want to bring down the economy; they are just people who believe what most people currently believe; that the goals of economic well-being and progress are best served by ever-increasing consumption of everything, and a few birds, bushes, and odd furry creatures are of no consequence by comparison.

In fact, of course, the ever-increasing consumption of resources and the elimination of species and habitats go against the goal of economic well-being, which is best served by environmental conservation and enhancement.

Visual and Noise "Pollution"

In terms of physically damaging, poisoning, or depleting the earth's living environment, there are no such things as visual and noise pollution.

These are red herrings in the sense that, for example, people who object to the noise of rock music, traffic, or children at play, or object to the replacement of an ornamental old building by a stark new one, feel entitled to attach their cause to the environmentalist cause (feeling licensed by the use of the word "pollution" in describing what they object to), thereby distracting attention from issues of real importance to the living environment and diverting energy that should go into resolving those issues in the environment's favour.

This does not mean that noise control, preservation of pleasant old buildings, and restriction of huge billboards may not be useful causes in their own right. But they should be fought separately, not used to burden the environmental movement whose job is so vital to economic well-being and thus to human welfare and survival.

It would be better if the word "conservation" were only applied to living things and their habitats, while the word "preservation" were applied only to inanimate human artefacts such as old buildings, machines, and artworks.

The reduction of economic activity through environmental degradation takes place in three ways—one direct and two indirect.

Several examples will illustrate the direct effect.

Failure to conserve topsoil reduces food production from plant and animal sources.

Failure to conserve forests destroys timber workers' jobs and reduces wooden goods in the economy. Of course "they" can find substitutes for wood, but this involves increased throughput and eventual depletion of some other resource.

Allowing plant and animal species to become extinct reduces the genetic diversity necessary to maintain the vigour and ensure the continued fertility and adaptability of all life on which humanity ultimately depends.

Using practically nonrenewable fossil fuels, coal, gas and oil, at rates far higher than could be accommodated using renewable energy sources, threatens economic dislocation. What to do about fuel consumption will be examined in a later chapter entitled "Nonrenewable Resources—Leave Them in the Ground?"

A mainly indirect adverse effect of environmental depletion on the health of the economy arises from the small component added to the rate of price increases by the depletion of so many resources, resulting from their throughput rate exceeding their renewal rate. The emergence of this point necessitates a digression to discuss depletion and inflation.

Depletion and Inflation

Throughput of resources, a first derivative of wealth, is of two kinds, gross and net. Net throughput is the flow of goods and services in the economy. Gross throughput is net throughput plus the resources required to extract and process wealth into those goods and services.

As resource depletion proceeds, net throughput becomes

an ever smaller fraction of gross. This is because the wealth base depletion forces the need for ever more work, more resource throughput, to realise each unit of goods.

If an area of sea is so depleted in fish that far more work than formerly required becomes necessary to get each fish, the money price of fish increases. But this price-increase factor is not true inflation (which will be defined later). It is a component of the second differential of wealth, that is throughput increase (TI). It is the rate of change of the ratio of gross-minus-net throughput to net throughput. It shall hereafter be called value inflation because, other things being equal, a unit of goods, even if it stays exactly the same, becomes more valuable as the throughput necessary to bring it to market increases, and this value increase must be reflected in an increased money price. But this is not the same as money inflation, the decrease in the value of money. In value inflation, the money may hold its value but the value of the goods is increasing.

The effect of improving technology is to reduce the value inflation rate by enabling, up to a point, a progressively more efficient extraction, transport, and processing of wealth into goods and services. That is, in the steady state where throughput is no greater than renewal, improving technology can cause a negative value inflation rate.

Where the throughput rate exceeds the renewal rate, improving technology can to some extent, and up to a point, counteract the restrictive effect of the shrinking of the wealth base.

However, technology itself requires throughput to develop and maintain it; and if resources are being depleted, then technology must improve at a rate sufficient to balance out the effect of this depletion. As depletion proceeds, the rate of improvement in technology must tend towards infinity. This is clearly impossible and nothing can stop throughput from eventually beginning to decline as resources are steadily depleted by the throughput rate continuing higher than the renewal rate.

Two further short points can be made here. First, technology can increase a renewal rate up to a point. Second, the rate of improvement of technology is slowed, not increased, by declining economic health.

After this digression, the discussion of the effect of environmental depletion on economic well-being continues.

Value Inflation—the Trigger, Not the Bullet

The direct addition of value inflation to the rate of price increases is quite small. The larger effect arises from secondary influences, in whose shaping human psychology plays an important part. These influences are triggered by the small value inflation component and its corollary, a slowing of the rate of net throughput increase relative to gross TI. These secondary influences are self-reinforcing.

Expectations have been for decades and continue to be that material living standards should continue to rise at a certain rate. Thus the effect of a slower rate of net TI and an accompanying boost to the rate of price increases is to create pressure from the people to close the widening gap between expectations and reality.

Several developments result.

Pressure for increased money wages, and increasing expertise and militance of workers' unions and associations, transfers money from profits and accumulated money capital to wages and salaries. The ratio of savings to total money

33

income falls as more money is diverted to purchasing goods and services immediately.

The ratio of money borrowing to income rises as people try to make up the difference between what they can buy and what they think they ought to be able to buy.

Governments borrow more to meet rising public sector wages, welfare transfer payments, and construction and procurement costs without politically impossible tax increases.

The private sector borrows ever more to meet the ever increasing amount of investment required, because of the increasing difference between gross and net throughput, to structure each unit of goods and services and to improve technology so as partly to counteract the effect of wealth depletion.

With borrowing rising faster than saving, the rate of increase of the amount of money available for investment falls behind the rate of increase of borrowing demand.

True inflation is boosted because the number of money units available for spending on goods and services rises faster than the flow of goods and services, so ever fewer goods and services are commanded by the same number of money units.

Interest rates are forced up by growing pressure on loanable funds and by increased inflation.

If governments were to increase direct taxes as well as borrowing more, this would reduce take-home pay and people would then feel a need to borrow more. This upward pressure on borrowing would be worsened by downward pressure on savings. Increasing indirect taxes through purchase tax or VAT would discourage consumption and borrowing while encouraging the accumulation of loanable funds in the form of savings and reducing the need for government borrowing. It would also slow resource depletion. More will be said on taxes in another chapter.

Implied in the last paragraph is the belief that people's expenditure is to an important extent determined by what they think they ought to have rather than what they can afford.

The marginal efficiency of capital, a quantitative expression of business confidence and a function of expectations, falls because of rising inflation and interest rates. This puts downward pressure on investment in new ventures in economic activity, or new investment in existing ones.

Jobs are eliminated by money wages rising faster than the money value of goods and services being structured. The jobs made vacant are either neglected or done by fewer workers using greater mechanization, more sophisticated structuring technology. This job attrition is particularly marked at the lower end of the labour market, the lower skill and lower value jobs. Jobs and their loss will be discussed again in other chapters.

Finally, the proportion of money flowing through the wages channel in the economy increases relative to the proportions flowing through the other channels. This moves the economy further away from the optimum proportionate flow status. This subject, proportionate flow, will also be discussed in more detail in other chapters, "Proportionate Flow Theory Applied to Wages; the Great Depression" and "Proportionate Flow Theory Applied to Wages; Modern Stagflation."

The effect of all these depressive influences is to reinforce themselves and each other by exacerbating the cause—living standards falling behind expectations.

So we have the "stagflation" of recent experience—unemployment, interest rates, and the rate of price increases all high together due to the same seed cause—the conflict between the limits to the earth's wealth on one hand and, on the other, the chase after the realisation of expectations of endless steady rates of throughput increase.

Stagflationary phenomena will also be discussed in other chapters.

Living Standard and Quality of Life

Another indirect adverse effect of environmental degradation on economic well-being arises from the effect of the degradation on people's perception of their economic condition.

A further illustration of the erroneously perceived conflict between environmental conservation and economic well-being lies in this frequent reaction to some piece of environmental devastation: "Oh well, at least it creates jobs for some people who wouldn't have one otherwise."

Certainly the degradation will keep some people busy for a while, but because of the depletion of the resource on which their jobs depend, there will be a net loss of jobs. This is easy to demonstrate in the case of forests, topsoil, and whales. But what of the less easily quantifiable environmental resources of a pleasant suburb, a clean recreational beach, a lovely view, a peaceful holiday island?

Say several kilometres of clean recreational beach are rendered useless for that purpose by some project that keeps a number of people busy for a year or two. The conventional view is that the money paid to the workers increases "the national income" and makes the whole community richer.

Actually it is the national throughput rate that is increased by the addition of the land, including the beach and whatever other resources are associated with the project, to the throughput activity. Beauty and amenity could also be regarded as resources added to the throughput activity.

The loss of the beach amenity will have several effects.

First, people accustomed to enjoying the beach directly, and those who enjoyed it indirectly by choosing to live near a beach rather than near whatever is taking its place, sense a lowering of living standard. This adds to the general pressure for higher wages because it widens the gap between expectations and reality where living standards are concerned.

The beach amenity was part of people's living standard but not in the same sense as the material goods and services they consume. It was part of people's "quality of life." This term is used here to mean that component of living standard that is hard to measure in money terms, being emotional and subjective rather than material. But the loss of a portion of quality of life is felt as keenly, and reacted to as forcefully, as the loss of the ability to consume some quantity of material goods and services.

The increased upward pressure on wages is accompanied by increased debt, rising interest rates, worsening ratio distortion (for explanation of that term, see the chapters on "Proportionate Flow Theory"), and, in fact, a similar self-reinforcing syndrome of economic aches and pains to that which flowed from the appearance of value inflation discussed earlier.

Also, land and housing prices are likely to change drastically in the vicinity of the lost beach. They may be sharply depressed. This causes people to sell up before they otherwise would and increase demand for land and housing in other areas, putting upward pressure on real estate prices there. So, many people will suffer a money loss between selling the old place and buying the new. Their financial difficulties will put increased pressure on loanable funds and tend to increase interest rates. Also the new area may have less environmental amenity than the previous one in its former condition. The two factors will combine to increase the general upward pressure on interest rates.

Alternatively, rezoning of the land to industrial use may raise the land price well above what is normal for house and garden purposes and drive the resident away through commercial pressure and higher rates. A good money profit will be made by people in this case, which will make it easier for them to buy a home elsewhere. The extra demand and the extra money in some people's pockets will have the effect of driving up residential land prices for everyone, with a consequent increase in interest rates and in debt as people still strive to buy land in quantity and quality to match their expectations. The raised land prices in one area spill over into other areas.

The fact that land and environmental amenity are limited resources is responsible for and demonstrated by the problems just described. The throughput of land and of building material is increased by the residential shifts. They don't make the country any bigger or richer.

More short-term jobs are created by the flurry of resettlement. But with the increased depletion rate of the wealth base and all the economic stresses set up it is arguable that more long-term jobs are lost than short-term ones created, leading to a net loss of jobs in the final working through of the initial blow of the loss of the beach.

The purpose incidental to which the beach was destroyed varies, depending on its nature, in its effect on direct short-term and indirect long-term employment.

If the beach was mined for mineral sands, this resource will increase employment in other places and ways during the time taken for it to be throughput, degraded, and dispersed. Another limited resource has had its throughput rate increased, and in this case its renewal rate is low. Jobs that depend on this resource will be at risk as it is depleted; this statement raises questions that will be examined later.

Or the beach might become an area reserved for the use of a relatively small number of people at a high money price. The beach is not destroyed, but is lost to the previously large number of users as effectively as if it had been. The effect is mainly to transfer throughput from some people commanding a disproportionate share thereof to others similarly placed, with little finding its way to less perfluent people.

The direct effect on throughput is minimal but the indirect

effects, through the perceived lowering of living standards of large numbers of people, are depressive as described above.

It often happens that a beach close to and used by large concentrations of people becomes unusable because of increasing pollution from expanding industrial installations nearby. The pollution itself creates no short-term employment and destroys other wealth as well as the clean beach. The industrial processes causing the pollution create short-term employment but boost the throughput of numerous limited resources, probably depleting them in the modern situation where so many resources are being throughput at a rate higher than their renewal rate.

Some questions raised by the foregoing paragraphs:

Is increasing throughput always bad? Jobs depend on maintaining resources, but how can there be jobs without throughput? Must it be "hands off everything"?

The answers will be discussed in the following digression.

Digression—Resource Consumption, Jobs, and "Hands Off"

Is increasing throughput always bad?

Not necessarily. Many times in this book, the reduction of throughput is stated or implied to be a benefit. But this only applies to present-day conditions when so many resources are being depleted because they are throughput faster than they can be renewed. Under these conditions increasing throughput of any resource will probably either accelerate its depletion rate or, if it is not yet being depleted, restrict the possibilities for using it (up to the limit that its available renewal rate allows) in place of resources that are being depleted. Thriving economic activity can go on indefinitely without resource depletion as long as the throughput rate stays below the renewal rate. So increasing throughput is good in circumstances where most resources are being consumed at a rate far less than the available renewal rate. In these circumstances increasing throughput is a benefit because the increasing level of economic activity that results can support more people at a better standard of living.

No, there cannot be jobs without throughput. Jobs are based on wealth, but are realised by the throughput of the wealth. Wealth must be conserved, that is its quantity maintained or increased in order to provide a secure future for jobs and economic activity; but the wealth must be throughput to enable the jobs to be performed and the economic activity to take place.

If the throughput rate of a resource that is already being depleted is further increased, this will provide a gain in short-term employment in exchange for a greater loss of long-term employment.

Short-term and Long-term Employment

That raises the question: Short-term or long-term, isn't any employment increase a permanent, "bankable" one?

No. "Short-term employment" describes the work directly entailed in undertaking a process. "Long-term employment" describes the work available in the total economy once the direct and indirect effects of that project have worked their way through.

Another way is to look at short-term employment as a cause whose effect is found in long-term employment. The effect may be loss or gain, depending on whether the short-term employment was active in depleting resources, conserving them, or increasing them or their renewal rate.

Current economic theory and practice places too much emphasis on throughput, neglecting the conservation of wealth, assuming resources to be unlimited. There are some at the other extreme who place too much stress on conservation, wishing to minimise throughput. This brings us to the next question.

Must it be "hands off everything"? Definitely not. There are some in the conservation movement who wish altogether to ban the throughput of certain resources, such as whales. The argument is that whales are beautiful and special and ought to be left alone.

All life forms are beautiful and special in their way but all animals must consume other life forms to survive. There is no choice about this.

A more practical approach to whales would be to leave them alone long enough for stocks to build up, then to crop them at a carefully controlled rate less than or equal to the rate of maturation (not reproduction—mortality before sexual maturity must be considered). The longer the whale "resource base" is given to build up, the larger can be the whaling industry, and the greater the rate of throughput and the number of jobs it can support when cropping resumes (but see Note on Whaling below).

The same kind of policy could be applied to forests. These are being rapidly depleted around the world, and the sensible thing would be to halt timber-getting and other encroachments and allow the forests to build up. But this would take centuries. A more practical policy would be to exploit the forests at a rate just below the renewal rate.

(The renewal of rain forests would require a very low level of cropping and careful land management to prevent erosion during renewal. A surviving large tract of virgin forest would be essential to enable the renewal to take place.)

This would allow the resource to build up slowly while still supporting economic activity. This policy could be generalised to every renewable but diminishing resource—and currently that means a host of different resources. People would need to be carefully taught that the restricting of economic activity resulting from the practical application of such a policy would be actually by far the lesser of two evils as far as jobs and living standards were concerned. The alternative, allowing unchecked exploitation, would cause a greater and more permanent loss of jobs and reduction of general well-being.

Note on Whaling

It is arguable that whaling makes available nothing that could not be obtained from plants such as olive or jojoba, from plentiful marine life forms, or land animals currently part of normal farm stock and in no danger of extinction. The unique properties of whale oil could not perhaps in former times be found or created in oil from land plants, but modern chemical technology can change the nature of any oil or synthesise any oil entirely from simple starting materials.

"When the Boom Comes"

For years governments and people generally in the more perfluent nations have been waiting for an economic "upturn" or "recovery" to reduce their now chronic high unemployment. The underlying assumption is that the high throughput increase rates, the so-called "economic growth" rates of the 1950s and 1960s, were normal and that the more sluggish TI rates of more recent years are an abnormal phenomenon that can be expected to speed up in time through this or that brilliant policy initiative or going back to the early economics of the eighteenth and nineteenth centuries; or by eliminating (depending on your viewpoint) businessmen, unions, migrants, taxes, civil servants, or computers; or just by waiting. Finally the upswing will come and get us all back to "normal."

This insistent looking forward to a mythical "boom" misunderstands the reasons for the present state of things and ignores the limited, though abundant, nature of the world we live in.

The effect of the world's limits on the economic history of recent years has been discussed earlier. What would be the effect of a boom, a large increase in the TI rate, assuming it could be achieved?

The rate of wealth depletion would increase. The technology improvement rate would also increase, and this, by improving the ratio of net to gross throughput, would delay the adverse effects of wealth depletion or cause that ratio to fall more slowly than it otherwise would. But, as previously shown, technology improvement cannot enable an indefinite increase in the rate of throughput of limited wealth. Nor can it enable the sustaining of a rate of throughput greater than the rate of renewal. Improving technology can, of course, by enabling substitution, increase some renewal rates, also reduce the throughput rates of some resources and increase those of other more abundant resources. But still there are limits to what technology can do in any sense.

Expectations would increase in every sector of society. This is not a hard objective variable, but it is of critical importance to the state of things and to the course of events.

43

In the hypothetical absence of rising expectations, if they could be "frozen," the increasing rate of wealth depletion would add a component to the rate of price increases. This component will be larger than it was before with a lower TI rate.

The increasing rate of wealth depletion in the more perfluent countries would reduce opportunities for increasing the rate of throughput in other countries. This would widen the already large difference between the per capita throughput rates of more and less perfluent nations.

Money prices for resources would rise, in many cases, out of proportion to the increase in demand or to any value inflation rate that may prevail. This would benefit resource-rich nations including many of the less perfluent, in money terms, transferring throughput in their favour. But their wealth would be reduced and their opportunities for future throughput reduced because of the transfer of wealth to high-consumption nations.

The extra money would enable the wealth-exporting nations to transfer throughput in their direction by importing goods and services, but never as much in quantity, though more diverse in quality, than the exported wealth.

When this transferred throughput had been put through, consumed, used up, the resource-exporting countries would have suffered negative economic growth because much of the exported wealth would have been extracted faster than its renewal rate, leaving it depleted.

The more perfluent countries will have had their throughput rate and their appetite for wealth increased. They would need to inflict more economic shrinkage on countries, including their own, where wealth is extracted.

An important point here that has been stated before and needs emphasis is that the process widens the gap between the deprived people of the world and the minority of high consumers. So the boom, if it ever comes, is to be dreaded, not welcomed, by the less perfluent nations; whatever short-term increase in throughput they may enjoy will be at the cost of less opportunities for throughput in the longer term.

The boom would be self-limiting even if expectations remained frozen. The steady depletion of wealth accompanied by a fall in its renewal rates and a rise in value inflation (the component of price rises caused by the increasing gap between gross and net throughput) would combine to cause rising economic stress and dislocation that would alleviate their cause.

The point here is that the world economy will certainly settle down to a steady state one way or another, whether by deliberate policy or by constraint of nature. The latter would be far more unpleasant for us and leave the world in a far worse state than the former. That is why the former is advocated. Of course it is always harder to do something involving politically unpopular steps than to sit back, let things drift, and blame the consequences on some popular target.

Another thing to note here is that the results of the hoped for boom, so far described, are the same as what has been developing anyway for several decades. The "economic recovery," as that term is currently understood, would merely make it happen more quickly and probably more distressingly. So its actual effect would be quite the opposite of what governments everywhere believe and hope for. A true "economic recovery" would be progress towards a sustainable steady state economy, and that is what we must hope and work for.

The Effect of People's Expectations

The factor of people's expectations, left out of this discussion so far, would change the outcome somewhat.

The effect of rising expectations would be to stop the "boom" and return to familiar "stagflationary" conditions sooner than if resource depletion alone were the depressing factor.

The mechanism whereby this would take place is described in other chapters. In one way it is better for expectations to rise and have this effect because it puts a brake on the process of resource depletion with all its unhappy results. But it is said elsewhere in this book, and will not be denied here, that rising expectations in the more perfluent countries are a major obstacle to the achievement of a steady state or sustainable world economy, that is by deliberate policy measures rather than by default.

Rising expectations impede the steady increase in perfluence to which they look forward, but this is also blocked by the fact of the earth's limits. The rising expectations completely ignore these limits as if they did not exist.

If people could somehow be persuaded to recognise, understand, and take account of the fact that the earth's wealth is limited and that there must be a limit to the increase of throughput, then they would reduce their expectations.

But this reduction of expectations would enable the economic systems to work more efficiently, putting upward pressure on the throughput rate, with a consequent acceleration of the rate of depletion of wealth. So while rising expectations impede the attainment of rising perfluence, falling expectations of perfluence temporarily make it more attainable.

Governments can't go on fueling expectations until economic systems seize up, nor can they allow wealth throughput

46

to surge ahead of renewal rates until economic systems break down under intolerable stress.

In practice it is easier to let expectations rise than to educate populations about the limited nature of the earth's resources—apparently a most difficult concept for most people to understand. So rising expectations can save resources and buy time while this arduous education process goes on and policies are developed that take account of the earth's limits. Eventually a strong attack on expectations can begin without boosting resource depletion.

Hard Work—Virtue or Vice?

People working overtime for extra pay, or purchasing more goods more often, or performing any act that increases their rate of consumption may justify themselves or be justified by governments or the media with the argument (consistent with current economic thinking) that by doing so they are boosting the economy, creating wealth, giving employment to people.

Hard work for long hours with few vacations is made a particular virtue in some countries, being believed to lead to greater national wealth, a higher standard of living, and ever more jobs in those countries and others, with the "wealth" supposedly "created" flowing to other countries.

In fact, any increase in consumption increases the rate of throughput of resources. If resources are already being consumed faster than they are renewed, or if the increase in consumption is sufficient to cause the consumption rate of resources to exceed the renewal rate when it did not previously do so, then resources are being depleted faster than before or are beginning to be depleted. This actually shrinks the economy, destroys wealth, and reduces jobs in the long term (see foregoing digression).

What really happens is that up to a point a greater national throughput rate is achieved.

This increases the national living standard as long as the TI rate is faster than the population growth rate and the throughput is fairly distributed through the population.

An increasing throughput rate means an ever shrinking wealth base as the renewal rate is exceeded and, to the extent that it depends on the size of the wealth base, reduced.

This sets up stresses in the nation's economy that exert downward pressure on the throughput rate and on living standards and reduce short- and long-term employment.

Pressure is also exerted against the ability of less perfluent nations to increase their throughput rate. This comes back to the point discussed in the chapter "Global Inequalities in Wealth."

As well as depleting wealth in their own economies and thus making less of it available for everyone's throughput, the more perfluent economies make available to the others facilities for the structuring or realisation of goods and services that would not otherwise have been available and that increase their throughput rate and living standards in the short-term.

This further accelerates the global throughput rate, depleting wealth yet faster. This is not transferring throughput but, rather, spreading the economic stresses, the wealth base shrinkage, with inflation and net job loss and ultimate downward pressure on throughput, from more to less perfluent nations.

Instead of making more wealth available to less perfluent nations, quite the reverse happens; wealth becomes less available than it would otherwise have been. Those last six words are important because yes, more and less perfluent nations may all be increasing their throughput rate at the same time. The point is that the faster the more perfluent countries increase their wealth throughput rate, the more costly and difficult it becomes for the less perfluent to do likewise.

Global resource throughput has to be kept within the limits imposed by the renewal rates of the different resources. More perfluent countries must restructure their economies to maintain full employment regardless of changes in the level of economic activity, letting living standards fluctuate instead. This will set the stage for throughput to be reduced, resource by resource, to enable it to be increased elsewhere without the overall throughput rate for that resource exceeding its renewal rate.

The present course of world economic development leads to a cycle of weakening lifts and deepening crashes in throughput, first in the most perfluent nations and then in more and more of the others as, and if, their perfluence increases.

Work is a virtue up to a point. We must all earn our living and contribute to the throughput in which we take a share, not be parasites. But working harder and harder to realise and consume more and more goods and services becomes more and more a vice.

A person with a fleet of powerful cars and several huge houses grossly beyond his accommodation needs is not, as we are currently taught, someone to admire and to strive to imitate. Rather, such a person is an obscenity, a criminal against the welfare of fellow human beings and the health of the ecosystem, the two things of course being inextricably bound up with each other.

A person who has two or three jobs or works normal time plus overtime and shifts, doing little else but work, eat, and briefly sleep, in order to make and consume far more goods than if he just worked flat time, is not sacrificing his

49

strength and his social and family life in order to create better security and ease for himself in the future. In fact, he is contributing to faster erosion of economic security for himself and for everyone else.

Actually if we really desire economic security and well-being we should consume as little as possible, which means making as few goods as possible, which means minimising rather than maximising work.

That last point does not mean drawing a wage while slacking, sitting around and not doing the work that the wage requires. It means giving a fair day's work for the wage paid, but on that basis working only enough to earn enough to support a minimum of consumption.

If the more perfluent countries had followed this idea after World War II there would have been, of course, a slower increase of material living standards and a slower development of technology; but so what? Nothing would have been irretrievably lost, merely postponed. But we could have avoided the huge menacing intractable global economic problems of excessive debt, mass unemployment, extremes of perfluence and deprivation, worsening environmental degradation and resource depletion.

The "workaholics" are enemies of the community and must be discouraged, not admired and copied. Their hard work is not accumulating wealth at a faster rate, but consuming it at a faster rate. As has been said before, life is a business of throughput, not of accumulation.

Anyway, it's all very well to talk of what should have been done. But it wasn't done, so we must find some way to cope with things as they are. It is hoped that foregoing and subsequent chapters will indicate some future directions for the world.

Who Needs the Snail Darter?

A subtle, indirect but nevertheless important further way in which environmental depletion damages economic health is through the extinction of species.

A particular species may not be throughput directly in the sense that a particular economic activity is based directly on that species. Its depletion will not be immediately noticeable either in direct job losses or in value inflation. Its disappearance may not be sufficiently noticeable to cause any sense of lower quality of life and thereby add to pressure for higher wages.

A classic case is that of the snail darter, a small species of fish in the United States of America.

The building of a huge dam was held up by an environmental law that barred any new development whose effects would include causing the extinction of any plant or animal species. In this case the habitat of the snail darter would be altered by the dam to such an extent as would threaten survival of the species. So the dam project appeared to be blocked.

This caused an uproar because compared with the economic "growth," jobs, "wealth," which people thought likely to flow from the dam, what possible benefit could result from skipping the dam and conserving the small fish?

The dam went ahead in the end because current economics contains no plausible answer to this question.

However, apart from the fact discussed previously and later that the dam would generate not wealth but throughput, not growth but throughput increase, far-reaching and devastating economic effects can flow from the disappearance of a species. Causes and effects are often separated by large time gaps with effects developing and causing other effects over an indefinite period rather than a cause taking place, having an effect, bang, at a particular time, after which people can say "Well, that's over."

It is timely to point out that the general ecosystem and the human economic system are part and parcel of the same larger entity, and while they might need to be treated separately for convenience, this separation is artificial and they are not in fact separate. What affects the ecosystem affects the human economy. The health of the parts depends on the health of the whole, and that of the whole on the health of the parts in any living organism. But this simple tautology is only valid if we are careful what is meant by health. Indefinitely expanding activity of any part at the expense of and without regard to the other parts is not health of the part and cannot promote health of the system.

The effects of the demise of the snail darter may not be known for some time. But a couple of examples can be given where the loss of a species (that is its loss by terminal extinction rather than by evolution into derived species) has had substantial adverse effects on actual and potential economic activity at a later date.

Individual members of the two species to be mentioned are much larger than an individual snail darter but this has little to do with the point being made here.

Beavers in North America were long regarded by forest industry and farming interests as a useless nuisance in economic terms, clever and interesting though beavers might be. These creatures built dams, limited water flow through forests, created beaver ponds. They were seen as interfering with human plans for water flow and usage and as obstructions to farm and forest industry machinery.

Beavers were thus shot for their fur, driven away, their habitats disrupted, and their work destroyed. Eventually large areas of forest and countryside were beaver free and water flowed strongly into streams and rivers.

But the economy did not benefit from this reduction of the beaver species. The water table in forests was lowered, soil was eroded, nutrients were leached from the soil. Tree growth was stunted or trees died. Areas of land previously fertile and productive became flood-prone and suffered salt encroachment and topsoil and nutrient losses. The margins of rivers became more poorly vegetated, making them vulnerable to breakup and thus threatening extensive flooding and massive topsoil loss.

So the reduction of one apparently economically useless species did not clear the way for faster economic growth, more jobs; in fact it led to substantial economic shrinkage by the loss or depreciation of important economic resources.

The beaver species has not yet suffered terminal extinction everywhere and efforts are now being made, in the cause of real economic progress and growth, to regenerate beaver populations in areas where they were formerly large but more recently reduced or eliminated by human interference.

Another example is that of the baleen whale. This species has a direct and obvious economic importance as a crop, unlike the snail darter, but this is not the point here. The point is the place of the baleen whale in the marine food chain.

The baleen whale feeds by filtering sea water through a dense structure in its mouth (formerly the "whalebone" used in corsets) to reject large animals and admit small zooplankton, particularly krill, a minute but abundant crustacean. Large masses of small creatures dispersed through large volumes of seawater are thus concentrated into large, far more easily caught bulks of protein.

Overfishing of baleen whales has reduced their numbers to the point where extinction threatens. Apart from making it necessary to find other sources of the materials provided by the whale, this reduction of baleen whales has left no efficient alternative means of harvesting the rich krill resources of the ocean. The krill resource has thus become less available, although its quantity hasn't been reduced. Reduction in the availability of a resource is economic shrinkage, just as much as reduction in its quantity.

So in this example, reduction of the baleen whale species has not led to economic growth and jobs and progress and so on, but has caused economic shrinkage in two important resources—baleen whales and zooplankton.

More Dollars for Conservation?

So, environmental conservation must be the primary goal, and economic well-being depends on it—not the other way round.

That last phrase refers to the spurious argument that economic "progress" as currently understood, i.e., increasing throughput of wealth, provides money which can be spent on conserving the environment.

The value of money is not, in itself, mere metal and paper, but in the throughput taking place within the area covered by the particular money type. Money actually represents throughput. What the argument in the previous paragraph says, in effect, is that increasing the throughput of environmental resources makes it easier to conserve them. Put this way the argument is clearly nonsense. It only seems plausible in relation to the current misconception, mentioned already, that economic activity creates wealth.

Nonrenewable Resources—Leave Them in the Ground?

The principle of consuming resources at a rate no faster than their rate of renewal appears to be untenable in the case of resources whose renewal rate is almost zero, as is true of fossil fuels, gas, oil, and coal, also fissile uranium and thorium.

The mention of fissile materials necessitates examination of the "fast breeder reactor" whose promise tends to encourage a casual attitude towards energy conservation. This examination will take place in a digression after this chapter.

Are nonrenewable resources not to be used at all simply because their renewal rate is practically zero? This would seem nonsensical.

A better answer would be to examine all the uses to which nonrenewable resources are put and find ways of meeting these needs with renewable resources.

The renewable resources would need to be used no faster than their renewal rate and their use would not be able to deplete other resources by causing their renewal rates to be exceeded.

The next step would be to reduce the consumption of each nonrenewable resource until its consumption rate is low enough to allow it to be replaced totally by a renewable resource without exceeding the limits imposed by the criteria in the previous paragraph.

An important point is that the consumption rate would always have to be limited by the actual state of technology and the known availability of renewable resources at the time. Some people will say that all nonrenewable resources can be used as fast as possible because market forces will always be able to produce the technology and provide the materials to replace them at any desired level of consumption. Basing economic planning on this kind of nonsense rather than on actual existing conditions is not good enough when all people vitally depend on working, sustainable economic systems. No amount of technological breakthroughs or business brilliance can break the barrier imposed by the earth's limits. This has been discussed in the chapter "Depletion and Inflation." To sum up, consumption is determined by resource availability; current economics thinks it is the other way around.

The current belief that consumption creates wealth and makes economies bigger and stronger and that consumption must always be maximised to give any hope of full employment is the reason for the fingers-crossed attitude towards resource depletion. That belief is disposed of in other chapters. If it were replaced by a realisation that (i) maximised consumption actually undermines economies and destroys jobs, and (ii) a thrifty society with consumption not growing can still be a full employment society, then a more practical approach to the use of nonrenewable resources could follow.

Digression: Fast Breeder Nuclear Fission Reactors

This technology promises to expand the amount of fissionable fuel available from natural uranium by a factor of about 60. This doesn't change the nonrenewable nature of the total uranium resource, but it does promise to make it so abundant as to encourage a casual attitude towards energy conservation.

"Fast Breeding" consists in using the stream of neutrons released by the fission of readily fissile uranium 235 to "breed" fissile plutonium from the relatively stable, only

56

slightly radioactive uranium 238, which actually makes up 99.29 percent of natural uranium and cannot itself be used as nuclear fuel.

An atom of uranium 238 captures a neutron in a resonance capture. In doing so it becomes an atom of uranium 239. After this it can go two ways; it can lose the neutron to become again uranium 238, or it can lose merely an electron to become neptunium 239 which, in turn, over a longer period loses an electron from its nucleus to become plutonium 239, the fissile, fuel-usable isotope of plutonium.

The much more likely event on capture of a neutron by uranium 238 is the rapid loss of that neutron without any further change of the uranium 238 into higher elements.

If the layer of uranium 238 around the neutron-emitting nuclear fuel is made thicker, then each uranium 238 atom can have more "goes" at capturing a neutron and each neutron can have more "goes" at attaching itself to a uranium 238 atom. This will increase the chances of each uranium 238 atom becoming a plutonium 239 atom, thus increasing the "breeding fraction" that is the fraction of nonfissile uranium 238 converted to fissile plutonium 239.

In practice a breeding ratio of 1.2–1.4 should be obtained, meaning that 1.2–1.4 kg of plutonium 239 is obtainable for each kg of U-235 consumed. Evidence is lacking that a breeding ratio greater than 1 has actually been consistently obtained over a useful period with the fast breeder reactors currently operating.

Butler, Raymond and Watson-Munro in "Uranium on Trial," 1976, give figures indicating that up to that time a breeding ratio of only 0.01–0.02 had been achieved—far too low to make any difference.

Assuming that breeding ratios are now or ever can be greater than 1 and allowing for losses, up to 60 percent of the world's uranium could become usable as fuel in fission reactors instead of the 1 percent usable by conventional burner reactors. This 60 percent could eventually be made available even if the breeding ratio were only infinitesimally greater than 1, but the time needed to get it all would be longer than if the breeding ratio were 1.1, 1.2, or 1.4. The resource's quantity isn't affected but its availability, the rate at which it can be got hold of, falls as the breeding ratio falls towards 1.

If the consistent long-term breeding ratio (CLTBR) were always below 1, then the proportion of the world's uranium that could ever be obtainable as fissile fuel would never be as great as the maximum 60 percent quoted above. It would fall ever further short of 60 percent according as the CLTBR fell ever further short of 1.

If the best the world could achieve was a CLTBR of 0.75, which would be pretty good, the proportion of the world's uranium that could ever be made available as fissile fuel would rise from 1 percent to only 4 percent—a mere fourfold increase. If the CLTBR were only 0.5, still respectable, the increase would be only twofold, from 1 percent to 2 percent. These figures can be checked using a sort of negative compound interest—1 kg breeds 0.5 kg, which breeds 0.25, and so on.

Fast breeder nuclear reactors cannot be seen as the path to a laid back paradise of unlimited energy consumption and no conservation effort.

Minerals in National Parks—Leave Them in the Ground?

The extraction of minerals often leads not just to the consumption and depletion of the mined material, but also to the unintended but unavoidable consumption and depletion of rich and vitally necessary biological resources, which are quite wasted in the process. This happens when minerals are located in nature reserves and national parks.

All the earth's resources, animal, vegetable, and mineral, should be usable for the human economy according to the limiting criteria set forth in this book. Parks and reserves are certainly conserved by banning mining in them, but this is not satisfactory because it locks up the mineral resources and causes negative attitudes to the conservation of biotic resources, with consequent careless destruction of them in impatient "breakouts."

A better idea is to permit mining in nature reserves within limits imposed by the overriding requirement to renew the biotic resource at a rate equal to or greater than the rate at which mining depletes it.

Great extra care would be necessary to conserve the biotic resource while getting the mineral. The rate of mining would have to be restricted and much work done to save the life species and restore the land, not necessarily to its original form but to a condition that would permit the survival and strengthening of all the life species originally there.

All this would involve the outlay or loss of money, but this is not a "cost," rather a transference or delay of throughput. This is discussed in the chapter "Costs—What Really Costs Us and What Doesn't?" and elsewhere.

Current mining methods, where overlying biotic resources are left out of consideration altogether, are more costly than what is proposed because they entail faster depletion of resources, that is, faster economic shrinkage.

So how is the money to be provided to pay wages for restoration and recovery work and to compensate for the restriction on the rate of extraction and sale of minerals?

As discussed elsewhere, the conservation of resources available to the whole community is required, and the necessary monetary effort must be shared by the whole community. It is unfair and impractical to load it all onto the mining company.

Restoration work should be paid for out of general revenue, which can be augmented for the purpose by taxes on unnecessarily high consumption of nonrenewable resources, such as motor spirit from fossil oil, or on unhealthy nonessentials like alcohol, tobacco, gambling, and junk foods.

In addition, mining companies would be subsidised to an extent sufficient to enable them to mine, pay wages, turn a profit, and compete with less restricted miners elsewhere.

With the development of world political and legal unity also called for in this book, and with growing awareness of the vital economic necessity for conservation of the living environment, mining companies in more and more parts of the world would be subject to the operating restraints set forth above and the need for subsidies to keep restricted companies competitive with unrestricted ones would decrease.

The foregoing paragraphs really point up how different the economics of the future must be from current economics. Several sacred "laws" would be violated by the proposals made in this section: The law of the survival of the fittest, the most competitive companies surviving. The law that money income must be maximised and outlay minimised. The view that companies must bear the entire cost of their operations. The supposed need for governments to keep out of things in general and particularly not to subsidise anyone. The supposed need for less regulation and restriction of economic activity, not more. The law that more and greater taxes are always bad. The law that if something can't be done by the private sector it's not necessary or desirable. Not to mention the different concept of "cost" that will develop as the book goes on.

Population and Wealth

A recent magazine article cited, as one reason for improving safety in the home and reducing deaths and injuries to children, the argument that the deaths and injuries were a cost to the nation because of the loss of "production" of goods and services which those children, had they become healthy adults, would have accomplished in their lifetime.

The loss of or damage to the children was thus seen as an economic "cost" to the nation which made it "poorer" than it could have been.

Of course we must never take less than the greatest care of our society's children. But the fact is that what those unfortunates would have achieved would have been throughput, not production, of wealth. A person's whole life is a process of consumption, not accumulation of wealth.

In economic terms, the tragic loss of those children actually represents a saving, due to less throughput and slower depletion of wealth. This comes back to the point that people are agents of wealth throughput, not creators of wealth. The goods and services not structured by the children who were never able to take their place in the work force are not irretrievably lost; the wealth that would have gone into them is still there and may be made into goods and services later on. It is not a case of a great pile of human-created wealth being everlastingly smaller than it might have been had those children lived a normal working life.

The article's argument is based on the misconception that people are a resource which may be harnessed to greater or less effect to create wealth. A nation with a greater population is assumed to be actually or potentially a wealthier nation.

In fact, people and their economic systems are part of

the total ecosystem, a part that draws its activity from through-putting the other parts and depends on their size and health for its activity. More people, more throughput, eventually depletes the other parts, reducing the activity of the human component. There must be a limit to the human population consistent with the limits of the other parts of the ecosystem. There may be arguments as to what the limit should be, and one determinant is the level of world economic activity which it is desired to sustain. But there must be a limit.

More in relation to this subject will be said in the chapter "Stabilising the Human Population." The concept of cost also requires further definition and analysis and this will take place in the chapter "Costs—What Really Costs Us and What Doesn't?"

Capitalism versus Communism

Another misleading idea is that capitalism and communism represent opposite extremes, opposite poles of economic theory and practice.

Many proponents of communism believe, inter alia, that if only the world were communist there would be no more environmental degradation, no more pollution, no more problems in that area.

A regrettable recent tendency has been for environmental conservation movements to become subsumed into the political "left" so that advocates on this side of politics regard themselves as the only legitimate spokespeople for environmental matters, and conversely many environmentalists feel obliged to support general left-wing causes and to side with communist and socialist nations in the ongoing world political and ideological wrestling.

The next step has been that many environmental movements have become mainly left-wing activist groups with conservation issues pushed into an inferior position and warped and chopped to fit the political causes. This will often put the environmentalist in the position of supporting some action which points in quite the opposite direction to a healthy ecosystem and a sustainable world economy.

On the other side, some environmentalists have become captured by the business lobby, giving rise to a movement for "sustainable growth," whatever that means.

A better view of world economics is perhaps that capitalism and communism, and the various hybrids in between, are but different varieties of one economic philosophy, the conventional, traditional flat earth economics. The assumption common to all is that the earth is a limitless source and a bottomless sink; or rather, that the question of whether the earth is or is not these things is irrelevant and need not be considered.

The difference between capitalism and communism is in their emphasis and practice rather than in their essential nature. More will be said on this in two following digressions.

Digression—Flat Earth Economics; Capitalist and Communist Varieties Contrasted

Communist systems cannot be maintained without coercion and authoritarianism, which tends to exclude the great majority of the people from participation in administration and policymaking.

63

Communication with the governed is restricted because suggestions for change or adjustment of policy are regarded by the government as criticism and therefore as a potential threat and as an act of daring, best not undertaken, by the governed. Any responsiveness by the government to suggestions from the people is seen as a sign of weakness that could open the gates to a flood of criticism and protest.

Since rigid ideology must always prevail, though much of it be in conflict with the real world and with the actual behaviour of people and economic systems, much of the criticism would have to be rejected, causing further discontent.

This combination of repression, poor communication between government and governed, and theory that persists with the authority of religious dogma against changes in the real world and in knowledge and understanding of it, tends to make communist systems less efficient than capitalist at generating throughput and not able to achieve such high rates of TI, given similar circumstances.

But the ability of capitalism to generate higher throughput rates makes it more unstable, more susceptible to the economic stresses set up by pushing harder against resource limits, and, in trying to prevail, more obviously in conflict in its theory and practice with the limited nature of the world.

Thus the belief that environmentalists must side with the extreme political left may be a partial truth in that the world's resources and life systems would undergo slower depletion and degradation if the whole world were communist. But the resistance to change and the repression of ideas and criticism would drastically impede progress towards a new sustainable economic theory and practice, so that the ecosystem might fare worse in the end.

The degree of human freedom which capitalism for its most efficient functioning, must allow permits far more dissent, debate, and communication with governments so that new ideas can develop.

One essential characteristic of capitalism is that it must at all times strive to maximise the consumption of every possible resource. The aim of each individual company is to maximise the consumption of its goods. The maximisation is to occur in this part of the throughput chain. In structuring the goods, the money profit must be maximised, so the resource consumption entailed in the structuring must be minimised. However the resultant of all economic activities pursuing this aim is to maximise resource throughput. A company buying resources necessary for its operations will want to minimise their consumption, but the company selling those resources wants to maximise sales. Since both buyer and seller want to maximise consumption of their goods, the overall pressure is to maximise resource consumption.

This conflicts with the requirement of round earth, i.e., sustainable, economics, that the consumption of resources must be limited to the available renewal rate. The available renewal rate is the natural one plus the rate available from any human-made processes that are actually immediately operable, not just at the theoretical stage.

Similar remarks apply to communism, except that the requirement to minimise resource consumption per unit of goods structured disappears, since there is supposed to be no private profit or capital accumulation and selling prices of goods are determined very often not by the money cost of structuring them but by the government's idea of what people ought to be able to buy given their level of money income.

One consequence is a leak in the throughput chain in communist systems. This means that resources are throughput straight to waste matter without serving a term as usable goods on the way through.

Examples of this in the USSR and eastern Europe have

been well documented over decades. Up to half the USSR grain crop has been lost because there is no money profit incentive to maximise the percentage of grain that actually ends up in the silos. During harvesting, threshing, collection, and transport, much is simply dropped by the way.

Metal goods have been made far too heavy because of "production" targets based on the total weight of "production" rather than on the number of usable items made available.

Another consequence is a break in the throughput chain when goods are consumed faster than they are brought to market. One example is the Polish milk racket, reported in 1982.

The Polish government, for reasons of social idealism, decided that people should not have to pay more than the equivalent of thirteen U.S. cents per litre for milk. This was put into practice by heavily subsidising the cost of milk so that the government paid dairy farmers more than sixty cents per litre for the milk and made up the difference from general government revenue.

But unavoidable wage and other outlays caused milk to cost the dairy farmers up to a dollar a litre to make available. To keep selling to the government at far less than this would quickly break them.

So farmers bought much of their milk from the government at thirteen cents per litre and sold it back to the government at a profit of about fifty cents per litre, while selling milk they had actually produced themselves, at a cost to them of about a dollar a litre, to the government at a loss of about forty cents per litre. This practice enabled the farmers to enjoy a cash income for a while. It was a roundabout, cumbersome method of getting a production subsidy. However it broke down because to enable it to work, milk was being consumed faster than new milk was being made available for some time. The end of that road is obvious.

Many other examples could be given where socialist governments decide that the people shall have a certain level of access to goods and this must determine wages and prices, without regard to the money value of work and the money cost of making goods available.

What steps could have been taken to avoid the Polish milk problem?

The government could have taken over the dairy farms entirely and paid farmers a wage to produce milk which could then be sold at whatever low price was compatible with the government's social ideals.

What would have been the consequences of this?

First, the Polish government, already burdened with huge debts to western banks, would have been saddled with large extra outlays.

Perhaps they could repudiate the debts on the principle of redistributing "wealth" (in fact, throughput) from more to less perfluent nations.

This principle may be valid in theory, but in practice the precedent set by one major debtor defaulting and getting away with it would be disastrous for the world economy where there is so much debt. It would set off a wild binge of what can only be called stealing. To function, an economic system must have discipline and if this discipline sometimes goes against what's just and fair then the rules must be changed. But this change must come about by orderly means, not by violating loan contracts agreed to by both parties in good faith. Relief for almost unrepayable debt incurred under existing rules must be sought within those rules. This is discussed in chapters "Digression: Farmers and Miners in Trouble" and in "The Problem of Government Debt."

Repudiating the debts would be a good way not to get any more loans. Increased borrowing beyond ability to repay would have the same effect. Thus there must be a limit to government money outlays. This limit is a reflection of the ultimate limit on the world's wealth and capacity for resource throughput, just as the stresses on the world economy reflect the increasing stresses being imposed on the ecosystem.

Second, the payment of a fixed wage to milk workers regardless of the quality or quantity of product would lead to losses, leaks in the throughput chain, as with the USSR wheat harvest.

Raising the price paid to farmers so that it exceeds the money they spend to realise milk would enable them to make a living but would increase government outlays yet further and encourage inefficiencies by creating the expectation that the government will raise the price paid to farmers every time they complain about their cash flow and threaten to start the racket again.

Another way could be for the government to stay out of it altogether, save their money, and let dairy farmers sell to consumers directly or through retailers at prices consistent with the money outlaid to make the milk available. This would be against communist ideology but would probably work in the sense of getting supply, demand, realisation (production) cost, and consumer price into a sustainable relationship.

Some communist countries have compromised strict ideology by adopting this system for many commodities and their economies have escaped the problems of others less bold. China and Hungary are cases of this.

It may seem here that the great capitalist "truth" of letting the free interplay of consumers and producers optimise the availability and consumption of goods and services, that is, of being ruled by the "iron law" of the market place, is being advocated here.

Truth it is, but only a partial truth because it takes no account of the "iron law" of the world's limits.

Digression: "So Long As We Profit, Costs Elsewhere Aren't Our Problem"?

A fault of flat earth economics as practiced in free enterprise economies is that it chops a nation's economy into sections that are too often treated as being self-contained and independent of other sections. This is not a useful or realistic view. An economy's resources, economic activities, and people must be viewed as a whole. This whole must in turn be treated as part of the larger whole, the world economy.

An example will illustrate this point. In the southwest of western Australia a serious pollution problem currently (1987) arises from the processing of crude titanium oxide, rutile, into pure titanium oxide (TiO2) for many important uses. The process currently used is digestion with sulphuric acid to dissolve everything, followed by precipitation of pure TiO2 and discarding the remaining solution. A heavy load of sulphuric acid contaminated with iron and other substances must be disposed of each day and this is done by piping it to effluent ponds spread up the Leschenault Peninsula.

The pipes often burst or leak. Effluent seeps into ground water, attacks the substrata, and gets into the sea. Economic shrinkage, as defined earlier, actually occurs on the Leschenault Peninsula due to the destruction of marine and dune life and the degradation of both ocean water and fresher water in underground aquifers. Economic growth is the increase or improvement of resources.

There is a solution. Purified TiO2 could be made available at the same rate with far less effluent and less energy consumption if the chloride process were used instead of the sulphuric acid process. The chloride process entails the treatment of rutile to extract titanium in the form of titanium tetrachloride. This is liquid at normal temperatures, boils readily, and can easily be separated from the dry residue, harmless dust not hard to dispose of. The TiCl4 is rendered to pure TiO2 and the chlorine is available for recycling to the start of the process.

But the processing company says this is not good for them. It would take time and much money outlay to convert the process, and deprive them of cash flow because production and sales of TiO2 would stop during the conversion period. Also, the rutile would need to be of a higher grade, at least 70 percent, to be suitable for the chlorine process. The company would need a market for their product guaranteed to be much larger than at present in order to recoup their investment, make up for lost sales, and ensure the company's survival.

The company's point of view is that they can't be concerned about the dunes, fuel resources, the plant and animal life of the seas and dunes, or the poisoning of ocean and underground water. They are only concerned with the rutile, the TiO2 they produce from it, and the maintenance of a cash profit for the company.

(NOTE: This overblown idea of the importance of money is a fault of present economics. A more practical view of money would be as the least important element in the economy, in the sense that money should be treated as subservient to other things for whose benefit money should be manipulated and moved freely about.)

Current economics thinks the company's point of view quite reasonable and acceptable. The company are not to be blamed for going along with a flawed economic system. The system itself is not to be blamed for being flawed; progress occurs through a series of imperfect stages. But blame would be due to an attitude opposing change and progress towards a better system.

Such progress would be the development and teaching of a holistic view of the economy. The rutile, the fuel, the marine and coastal life and the aquifers would all be part of the resource pool. The TiO2-producing company would be one component of the economy's throughput mechanism. If there is a method of getting the same amount of pure TiO2 with less negative economic growth, i.e., less resource depletion, then this method must be introduced as soon as practicable. The particular throughput component, the TiO2 company, must be enabled to show favourable cash balances during and after the conversion period by purposeful manipulation of the money in the economy. The overriding goal must be to minimise the resource throughput entailed in realising goods and services or, to put it in terms already explained, to maximise the ratio of net throughput to gross throughput.

Capitalism versus Communism Continued

To come back to the subject of capitalism versus communism, the real extreme, the true opposite polarity, would be between flat-earth economics and a new economics, round-earth economics. The latter not only assumes the earth's capacity as a source and sink to be limited, but incorporates these limits as directly relevant and determinative in every sphere of economic life.

The great human leap forward that moving to such an economics would represent is comparable to that when it became generally accepted that the world was indeed a sphere rather than a flat disc; or to that which took place with the development of quantum and relativistic mechanics to supplant the Newtonian or classical mechanics that had served for two centuries.

In that case, Newtonian mechanics was not entirely wrong and served as a valuable foundation for later structures, but it was incomplete, failing to explain or predict ever more phenomena as the physical sciences developed.

Similarly, current economics is not totally wrong and contains many useful concepts and relations which can be incorporated, albeit modified and renamed, into the more highly evolved economics of the future. Current economics is just increasingly inadequate to explain, predict, or manage economic affairs in this ever more crowded, complex world economy.

The task of environmentalists must be to develop and move the world towards this new economics. To this end the environmental movement must be its own self, hold its integrity, subsume other movements and warp them to its own ends, cut across increasingly irrelevant barriers between "right" and "left."

The process whereby round earth economics can develop has been suggested earlier in the *Foreword* under "Evolution, Not Revolution."

Limits to Growth?

Current economics assumes a world of unlimited resources, unlimited wealth. No matter how rapidly a resource is used, either (i) "They" will always find more, or (ii) substitute resources will always be found to serve to any required extent as well or better in place of the depleted resource.

Such conditions would characterise a flat world extending indefinitely in every direction, clearly not the world we live in. In such a hypothetical world, economic systems of

72

any kind would be unnecessary. The very existence of economic systems on earth results from the fact that all resources, however abundant, are limited in five ways—in quantity, in potential extraction rate, in concentration, in accessibility, and in renewal rate.

Two kinds of limits may be defined; ultimate and potential.

The ultimate limits to a resource are, the total quantity, known to humanity or not; the concentration and distribution; and the limit to the possible rates of extraction, throughput, and renewal.

The practical limits at any time are the quantity known to exist with its known concentration and distribution, the extraction and throughput rates potentially available with existing technology, and the currently available natural and human-assisted renewal rate.

The practical limits can of course be extended, approaching closer to the ultimate limits, but never exceeding them. Current economics recognises some practical limits (though quite leaving out the renewal rate) but assumes that they can be extended indefinitely.

It is argued in other chapters that this false and indefensible, though usually unconscious assumption is at the root of much of the world's present economic trouble and dis appointment.

The throughput rate exceeds the renewal rate for many vital resources, as discussed earlier. There is only one way to a sustainable economy; limit the throughput rate of every resource to the currently available renewal rate. Maybe this would allow the limit to be raised from time to time, maybe it must fall steadily for a long time, but there must always be a limit.

If the quantity of a resource is large compared to its throughput and renewal rates but throughput exceeds renewal, the resource is being depleted. Its large quantity is no reason to continue this; it merely allows more time to reduce the throughput rate, allowing priority to be given to resources whose depletion rate is dangerously high compared to their quantity.

In the past, some have spoken of "Limits to Growth." This is misleading; actually there are limits to throughput. Economic growth, if redefined, need not be limited.

Economic growth is of two kinds: quantitative, as explained earlier, and qualitative. The latter is achieved by improvement in the ratio of performance to cost of goods and services, cost being measured in terms of resource throughput.

The same amount of material that made a simple calculator in 1973 made a pocket computer in 1983. Many diseases as time goes on can be cured more effectively with less effort and medication. More various and better quality polymers can be made from the same throughput of fuels and organic minerals compared with fifty years ago. Aluminum could once be made only with high throughput and labour for each kilo, but now it is (do not assume I approve) throwaway packaging.

All these are examples of qualitative economic growth, which has no definite limits.

The current understanding of economic growth, being in fact an increasing rate of throughput of wealth, is put forward as a solution to world economic troubles, but it clearly cannot be sustained and trying to force it to continue in the face of multiple resource depletion (actually = economic shrinkage) has actually caused current world economic troubles and will continue to aggravate them.

Economic growth as redefined in these pages would help the world.

Solar Energy—a Special Case

The term *solar energy* means not only the direct radiant energy of the sun, but also its stored forms—plants, animals, fossil fuels.

The sun's radiant energy is not a resource, but the result of throughput of a resource—that being the sun's matter. This is apparently nonrenewable and its depletion will ultimately mean the extinction of life on earth.

However: (i) this depletion will take such a long time as to be, for all practical purposes from a human point of view, eternity; (ii) there is nothing we can do about the throughput rate anyway.

At the point where the radiant energy is available for consumption, before further links are added to the throughput chain, it has no price, since no human agency or throughput of terrestrial resources is involved in bringing it to this point.

The human agency comes in when the radiation is to be converted to electricity or higher-grade heat, or used to bring about desired chemical reactions apart from natural ones. Terrestrial resource throughput also is required by this human terrestrial extension of the solar-matter throughput chain. So a money price must appear.

Money price is only associated with human-initiated resource throughput. Much terrestrial resource throughput arising from solar radiation has always taken place independent of the human race.

Most of the radiant energy reaching the earth from the sun, that is all except the portion lost through reflection and re-radiation, already serves essential needs for life and economic activity. It goes into:

(i) Maintaining the temperature of the biosphere within the range necessary to allow life to evolve and persist;

75

(ii) Driving the weather systems which allow fresh water to irrigate land masses;

(iii) Enabling processes of photosynthesis, weathering, decomposition and numerous biochemical reactions on which all life completely depends and without which no coal, oil, or gas would have accumulated.

Human throughput chain-links can be added without necessarily interfering with item (i). Capturing the energy and doing something else with it on its way through to becoming heat need not affect the earth's dynamic heat balance, provided that the amount of reflected or re-radiated radiation is not thereby affected. Even if it is, this need not be bad provided the biosphere is maintained within a certain temperature range; shifts up and down this range will merely alter climate patterns and the distribution and relative proportions of species.

Drastic changes in local climates could take place, however, if really large numbers of solar collectors became concentrated in a large city, where vast amounts of higher-grade heat would be generated from radiation that would otherwise be reflected away to the atmosphere and space. This problem still lies in the future.

Item (iii) should not be interfered with at all; it would be if large area solar collectors were permitted over areas that were anything but true deserts.

It is often said that solar energy is free, unlimited, and non-polluting. None of this is true.

It is only free until it is harnessed, then a money price must appear as discussed above.

It is not unlimited. The rate of flow and concentration of radiation have a limit that we cannot affect one way or the other. And there must be a limit to the harnessing of the radiation, not only because of considerations discussed above, but also because of limits to the terrestrial resources whose throughput is entailed in the process of obtaining heat, electricity, and fuel from solar radiation.

It is not pollution free, because the just mentioned terrestrial resource throughput would result in degraded matter that would be toxic or obstructive and would require reconstitution into renewed wealth.

The Solar-Powered Car

In a feat of courage, enterprise, and endurance, Hans Tholstrup drove a solar powered car across Australia in 1979. The car had a large flat roof arrayed with photoelectric cells that turned the sun's radiation into electricity and charged a battery.

Solar radiation cannot deliver more than about a kilowatt, roughly an old-fashioned horsepower, per square metre at ground level, and it usually delivers less. Allowing for the conversion rate of photoelectric cells, 10 percent to 25 percent, and the fact that the cells couldn't block in the whole roof area, then ten square metres, an unwieldy burden, couldn't deliver more than about a horsepower to the motor.

But the average petrol-driven car, whose normal function is to carry just one person, delivers about one hundred horsepower upwards. This is regarded as a "basic necessity." If this be true, then the directly solar-powered car is not feasible. But if one horsepower maximum is all you need to carry two people, as were carried in the 1979 trip, across a continent, then our transport needs could be met using such small amounts of liquid fuel as to make it forever unnecessary to lumber a huge collector about the place.

The Tholstrup car was nothing more than an entertaining irrelevance to the whole problem of evolving rational, sustainable energy policies for the future.

Money Supply, Throughput and Inflation

Material living standards are a function of three main variables—net throughput (Tn), population, and the prevailing distribution (D) of Tn among different social and occupational groups.

Tn is a function of available wealth, the state of technology, wealth renewal rates, human values, D, and the proportionate flow of money through different economic channels.

The value of money is determined by Tn and money supply. Increases in money supply greater than increases in Tn lead to devaluation of money. This and only this is true inflation.

Money is an agent of throughput in that its existence facilitates the exchange and consumption of goods and services which is Tn. However, as long as there is plenty, the actual quantity of money is irrelevant as a determinant of throughput. What is relevant is (related to D) the relative proportion of the total money supply flowing through different channels of the economic system—government, investment, wages and salaries, consumer spending, transfer payments, and savings.

Changes in money supply affect throughput but not because the overall quantity is changed, rather because the means of changing the quantity has always involved changing the relative proportions flowing through different economic channels.

78

An increase in the money supply isn't necessarily inflationary. That depends on its effect on throughput, since inflation only takes place if the money supply rises faster than throughput, or if throughput falls faster than the money supply. A fall in the money supply could be inflationary if that fall took place in such a way as to cause a greater fall in the throughput rate.

The statement that actual money supply is irrelevant as a determinant of throughput may appear to contradict the definition of true inflation, since the true inflation rate is one determinant of throughput, as will be discussed later.

There is no contradiction because the true inflation rate is determined by the relation between the rates of change of money supply and Tn. The rate of change, the first derivative of the quantity, is relevant; the actual quantity itself is not.

Real and Money Wages: Living Standards

Real wage and material living standard will be treated as different terms for the same variable.

The real wage, however, is not the same as the money wage. The real wage is the access to goods and services given to a worker in exchange for their labour. A change in the level of money wages is one determinant of a change in the level of real wages. A change in the overall throughput rate is another determinant.

Real wages always change as the direct result of movements in other variables. Money wages always change as the result of conscious, deliberate human decision, taken as a human response to changes in other variables.

A change in money wages must effect some change in

real wages because of its effect on the determinants of real wages. But a change in real wages does not change the money wage; only human responsive action can do that.

The change in real wages effected by a change in money wages may be in the same or the opposite direction to the money-wage change, and may be a greater or smaller percent change than that in the money wage.

Under present-day conditions, the following points apply:

If only one person receives a higher money wage, then their real wage will increase in the same proportion while having a negligible effect on that of others.

If a sizable minority of workers gets a money-wage increase, then their real wage may increase, but by a lesser percentage than that of the money-wage increase; and the real-wage increase will be at the expense of the real wage of other workers.

If the whole work force receives a money-wage increase, then everybody's real wage will decrease.

As we pass from the case of one worker getting more money to that of the whole work force getting higher money wages, the direct effect on real wages of having more money to spend becomes ever less important while the indirect effect on real wages, operating through the effect on the rates of throughput, inflation and interest, becomes ever more important.

A 10 percent increase in money wages does not guarantee a 10 percent increase in living standard. Under modern conditions, in the more perfluent countries, it guarantees a drop in living standard.

The effect of a change in money wages is to change the proportionate flow of money through the economic organism. Depending on what these proportions were before the change, and on whether prevailing economic conditions had

had time to reach an equilibrium with the state of those proportions, the effect on throughput may be to increase or decrease it.

In general, it could happen that a rise in money wages leads to a fall in real wages and, conversely, that a fall in money wages could increase real wages.

Digression: Caution about "Increases" and "Decreases"

These increases or decreases, it must be emphasised, would be not necessarily absolute, but relative to what real wages would have been, depending on other variables, if the money wage change had not taken place. It is necessary to be reminded constantly that we are dealing with an array of interdependent dynamic variables. This unavoidably complicates all considerations.

Because C, D, and XYZ are continually affecting A in their own way, it is not possible simply to say that if you increase B, A will fall.

It would be more accurate to talk of upward or downward pressure being put on variables.

If a rise in A puts upward pressure on B, B may still fall, but not as much as it would have in the absence of the rise in A.

This caution will need to be referred to at many other points.

Proportionate Flow Theory Applied to Wages: the Great Depression

The Great Depression of the 1930s has been very thoroughly gone over in the literature and there would be no need to mention it here except that it is necessary to describe it in terms of the concepts presented in this book and to link it with the present day.

Consider the case of the industrialised nations fifty years ago and today.

There is an achievable optimum relationship of wages to Tn. Wages rose more slowly than Tn for years after World War I, so that wages came to be too small a fraction of Tn.

However, a sustained "boom" of rapidly increasing throughput, enabled by new technology whose development had been stimulated by the war, caused rising expectations and a high level of confidence. These factors combined with the wage deficiency to give rise to excessive private borrowing and unsound speculation in an attempt to close the gap between cash income and desired purchasing power.

With too little money flowing through the wages channel, a spurious effect was created where money flowing through the consumer spending channel was more nearly sufficient in proportion to the other channels. The catch was that too much of this money that should have been wages was lent and had to be given back, with interest.

Businesses borrowed excessively too, not because their profits were too low, but because of the other two factors: expectations and confidence.

Eventually a point arrived where business and consumers' debt was so excessive a fraction of expenditure, and stocks and shares were so hugely overpriced, that the whole distorted structure crashed and collapsed.

A realisation that stocks and shares were grossly over-valued led to a selling panic that could not be stopped before near rock-bottom. Much of this stock had been bought on "margin," a form of buy now, pay later. This added to the huge load of debt that could not now be paid back.

Overborrowing had been accompanied by overlending, caused by the same high expectations and buoyant confidence. So banks found themselves with so much bad debt as to cause the loss of savings and accumulated profits.

Where did the money go? Much of it didn't exist. The collapse of 1929 stripped away the spurious apparent proportionate flows of money through the various channels and left the bare reality—too little money in the consumer spending channel, too much idle money not being borrowed or spent.

With people and businesses unwilling and in any case unable to borrow, very much inclined to save, and wages being generally too low compared to the value of work performed in exchange for them, there was downward pressure on prices.

This led to a drop in throughput, due to the operation of other variables that require goods and services to command a certain minimum money price to make their structuring worthwhile.

The falling throughput led to rising unemployment, further reducing aggregate demand and throughput itself. The throughput level is not, as currently believed, the sole determinant of the unemployment rate, but under the conditions of the Great Depression it was a major determinant.

An equilibrium was reached at a high level of unemployment, a low throughput rate not tending to increase, and wages for much of the working population not far above subsistence level.

Meanwhile, too much money had been flowing into the

savings channel—not because profits and savings were extraordinarily high, but because the rate of saving and profit accumulation was higher than the rate of lending for business investment, government spending, and private consumption.

"Boom" conditions and high confidence make people more inclined to borrow, and banks more inclined to lend, in the latter case even to a greater extent than their available funds would justify; while in Depression conditions, people are more inclined to save, even if this means scrimping on necessities; and banks are less inclined to lend, even if they are well funded.

Governments were committed to the idea of balanced or surplus budgets as the road to economic health, and were not willing to borrow. Business borrowing for investment was low, in line with the low marginal efficiency of capital.

At that time, there was in conventional terms "underconsumption." Put another way, there was a mismatch between two links of the throughput chain, between the structuring of wealth into goods and services and the subsequent use and degradation of these.

Of course the goods and services were not in general being structured faster than they were being consumed; the point was that the rate of consumption that aggregate demand made possible was lower than the rate of structuring of goods and services that available workforce, technology, loanable funds, and resources wealth made possible.

In the equilibrium state mentioned above, purchasing power was just sufficient to buy the goods and services being structured at prices just sufficient to keep them being made.

It was necessary to transfer money across economic channels, to free idle money piled up in banks, and place it in the hands of consumers to set idle hands to work preparing goods and services for market. But this had to be done not by lending the money to consumers as a debt to spend now and pay back later with interest, rather by providing the money as wages to spend as one's own money.

J.M.Keynes in his "General Theory" suggested that the money tied up in banks could be put in bottles and buried down derelict mines, after which the unemployed could be put to work digging it up. Their spending it would boost economic activity and lower unemployment.

The bizarre nature of this scheme would make it unacceptable as policy, but in the conditions of the Great Depression it would probably have achieved the desired result.

The task was to find a scheme equivalent in substance and effect, which had a more acceptable form.

Deficit Financing

The plan which eventually became acceptable, more readily under pressure of the Second World War, was that of deficit spending, whereby the government deliberately set out to spend more than they received through taxes, duties, and charges. The gap could be filled by borrowing, thereby mobilising stagnant funds.

Another way of closing the revenue gap is to print money. This actually increases the money supply instead of altering the proportionate flows of the existing supply.

Whether borrowed or printed, the extra money was spent on public employment, on increased doles and pensions, and on subsidies to particular industries or regions, or outright purchase of industries, or large government orders for goods and services from industries that otherwise would lack a market.

Whatever the source of the funds, the effect was to increase the flow of money through the wages channel relative to flows through other channels.

If the deficit money were printed, inflation need not necessarily result. It is not possible to state as a generalisation that printing money is always inflationary, or that it is never inflationary; or that the inflation, if any, is always in proportion to the money supply increase caused by the printing. The effect on money value of printing money depends on the economic circumstances in which the printing takes place, the state of the proportionate flows at that time, and on which economic channel the printed money is pushed into.

It could happen that the stimulus to throughput arising from printing and spending a new batch of money would increase the flow of goods and services sufficiently to match the increase in money supply, resulting in zero inflation from that source.

Supply-side Economics and the Laffer Curve

So-called "Reaganomics" practiced from 1981 by the Reagan administration in the U.S.A. was nothing more than a distorted Keynesian Great Depression policy practiced in the wrong context.

The theory was that large tax cuts would boost economic activity by giving people more money to spend on goods and services. A larger government deficit was seen as necessary in the short term, but this would be wiped out by increased tax revenues, at the lower tax rates, because economic activity would increase to such a large extent.

What happened was that economic activity increased for

a while, but the deficit grew to unprecedented size, to the point where just the interest on the cumulative debt owed by the government to the banks was the third largest item in the budget, after armaments and social welfare (see also chapter "The Problem of Government Debt").

This huge deficit can no longer be eliminated easily; even a determined, selfless effort by all branches of government will take years.

The brief, modest increase in the flow of goods and services was bought at the expense of a greater flow of goods and services in the future. The effect was to plunge the economy into a deeper recession, i.e., depress the throughput rate and its derivative to a greater extent than before, with unemployment yet higher in the absence of special action to give full employment maintenance priority over real wage maintenance (see chapters on Wages).

The famous Laffer Curve purported to show the effect on the federal deficit of reducing taxation. Instead of the deficit increasing indefinitely as taxation decreased, the curve showed the deficit increasing up to a point, then levelling off and falling as taxation was further reduced, due to the increase in economic activity out of proportion to the decreases in taxation that were supposed to cause it.

The assumptions behind this curve are consistent with those underlying the supply-side economics that formed the core of the Reagan administration's economic policy.

It is ironic that a policy of effectively increasing wages through larger government deficits, which would have led to increased economic activity and reduced unemployment in the Great Depression, should be tried in a different and inappropriate context fifty years later by a political party that fiercely opposed it during the Great Depression.

The Optimum Proportionate Flow Condition

To repeat in another way a point discussed earlier, there is an achievable optimum flow of money through the aggregate income (wages plus social welfare) channel in relation to the flow through other channels. The optimum state is characterised in two ways: (i) full employment, that is no involuntary unemployment of able people, prevails; (ii) economic activity, the wealth throughput rate, is at the maximum possible within the constraints imposed by other factors.

The optimum point cannot be determined by calculation or theoretical prediction; it can only be found by careful practical policies that change the proportionate flows in the right direction. Initially of course there must be a correct assumption as to the sense in which the proportions are distorted.

The pumping of money into the aggregate income channel was the right thing in the Great Depression—right in terms of the conditions in which it was proposed and the practical effect of the proposal as it eventually took shape as working policy.

The false assumption made by many is that it was the increase in the money supply generally sustained over a long period and the increase in consumer spending money as such that led to the increased economic activity and reduced unemployment. The erroneous inference drawn from this assumption was that any time unemployment rose and economic activity was apparently not increasing as fast as it could, the answer was to "boost the economy" with deficit spending aimed at increasing the money flow through the aggregate income channel. The assumption and the inference are referred to by too many supporters and opponents as "Keynesian." This label is a calumny.

The prolonged success of deficit spending policies was

due not simply to the fact that the money supply or consumer spending money were increased, but to the change in the proportionate flows which such increases brought about.

J.M.Keynes' proposals for lifting the Great Depression were not his theory as such; they were the particular treatments which his general theory showed to be appropriate for a particular type of economic malaise. The fact that these treatments don't cure our modern economic problems doesn't disprove the general theory. Rather it suggests that we must find other treatments, which could still be consistent with Keynes' Theory and would alleviate modern problems.

This was discussed further in the chapter "Proportionate Flow Theory Applied to Wages; the Great Depression."

Due to global resource limit factors, of which Keynes took no account, the answer is not that simple. This does not mean that Keynes' Theory was wrong as far as it went, any more than Isaac Newton's laws of mechanics were wrong as far as they went. These theories, and theories in general, need to be modified to accommodate knowledge and insights not previously available.

That last paragraph raises an issue that will be discussed in a digression, before dealing with the application of Proportionate Flow Theory to modern economic problems.

Digression—Thrift versus Spendthrift

Merely transferring money into the wages channel, increasing the spending power of consumers without forcing them to borrow, is of course not enough; the spending power must be translated into effective demand, with increased spending and consumption actually taking place—the more the better.

The resulting increase in the throughput of goods and services increases employment and also increases the rate of wealth depletion, bringing it closer to, or pushing it further ahead of (varying from one wealth form to another), the renewal rate.

Maximising consumption and its rate of increase have become the global economic religion since Keynes' time, with the old virtue, thrift, becoming a vice. Governments, and business through intensive advertising, have promoted the new creed as being good all round—higher profits, higher taxes, permanent full employment, everybody always getting richer.

Of course it would be good for all forever if we lived on a flat earth extending indefinitely in all directions. For most of history this concept would have been a good enough approximation to the actual round, limited earth we live on. But it is no longer good enough in the age of technological humanity, dominating the planet.

In fact ever-increasing consumption depletes more and more resources, eroding the whole basis of economic activity and setting up stresses, as described elsewhere, which push unemployment up again.

Thrift is necessary to use as little of a resource as possible and thus maximise the chances of having a sustainable economy that is in dynamic equilibrium with the world's resources. Another name for this is the steady state economy.

But this kind of thrift, in the absence of other measures, would have left the unemployed of the Great Depression in that state all their lives.

So that is the dilemma—the maximised consumption that lifted the Great Depression and whose continuation appeared necessary to keep employment full have, through resource depletion and its secondary effects, caused unemployment to rise to levels comparable to those of the Great Depression.

So what's the answer? What should have been done in the 1930s? What should be done now? The answer will be developed in the chapters that follow.

Proportionate Flow Theory Applied to Wages—Modern Stagflation

Misnamed "Keynesian" deficit financing policies applied in more recent years to "recessions" have contributed more and more to inflation and less and less to alleviating unemployment.

These policies have come to exacerbate the very disease, unemployment, they were meant to remedy.

About 1970, in the perfluent nations money wages began rising faster than Tn, having an ever larger ratio to it. This was a result of efforts to maintain, in an era of slower throughput increase, the rate of increase of living standards that had become familiar during two decades.

These efforts contributed further to the decline in throughput increase rate, TI, which had initially caused them to be made.

The decline in TI was triggered by the appearance and growth of a value inflation (see earlier chapter) component in the general rate of price increases. This has been discussed earlier with its consequences for throughput and other economic variables.

In consequence of this straying of proportionate flows of money away from the optimum, wages are now generally too large in comparison with profits, savings, and the money value of work performed. Before and during the Great Depression wages were generally too small in comparison to these things.

The rise in unemployment takes place in various ways.

Excessive Wages Can Cost Jobs

In the Great Depression and in the modern predicament, the work could be available to employ everyone if the money were available to pay them.

In the Great Depression, the money needed to come from the pile of inert money resulting from chronic excessive flow through savings and profit channels. Today it needs to come from excessive wages being paid to those working.

There is greater scope for this at the lower end of the wage scales. For reasons of social idealism and political advantage the lowest wages have undergone the greatest proportionate increases in recent years. Pressure for this also arises in more perfluent nations from the current policy, of those governments, that everyone must have their own car for all travel, to work or otherwise. The car's usual function is to carry just one person, yet a car has seating for four to six, weighs one to two tonnes, and has often well in excess of one hundred kilowatts of motive power. Clearly the minimum wage must allow for this unnecessary extravagance as well as food, clothes, and shelter.

The result is that many jobs, useful and having some economic value, have been eliminated or reduced as the wage required to be paid for them has leapt ahead of the money value of the goods and services made available by the performance of these jobs.

A positive stimulus to technological improvement is one result, as automation of work is introduced at a faster rate than would otherwise have been the case, to enable fewer workers to achieve the same level of structuring of goods and services or, in current terms, to increase productivity.

Another result is that many jobs are simply not done.

Collecting fares on public transport is useful but can be done by the driver instead of a separate person. This is increasingly the case as wages for fare collectors have risen way ahead of the money value of their work.

More salespeople in shops or shops open for longer periods would be useful and have some money value, but they can be done without as wages in the retail trade rise faster than money sales per worker.

Cleaning, caretaking, property-watching, repair, and maintenance are other jobs that are being neglected as more money than they are worth is being asked to get them done.

Rising wage cost of maintenance increases the number of cases in which it is cheaper to buy a new item than to repair the existing one, and thus increases the rate of throughput of wealth required for the same purpose, i.e., the use of that item for a given period.

A special example: the recycling of materials such as paper, cloth, metals, or glass would provide employment and reduce resource throughput by reducing the need to extract raw materials to make totally new supplies of these materials. Two important economic benefits would thus be achieved. This topic will be discussed in more detail a few chapters hence in "Digression: Renewal and Recycling of Resources; Wages and Jobs."

Of course some money loss results to the potential employer from not employing people in these jobs. But the point is that greater loss would result from employing them, since the company income resulting from their employment would be less than the outlay for the wages required to be paid them.

One determinant of the amount of employment possible at any time, is wage levels. This determinant can operate in either direction, depending on the state of the proportionate flows. In the modern context of the more perfluent nations, the relationship is always inverse—a rise in wages always exerts downward pressure on employment levels.

Many jobs are still done because they have to be. Not every job disappears as soon as the wage slightly exceeds the money value of the goods and services made available by the job. In practice there is some degree of buffering. A job's wage must be ahead of its value for some time, and the difference between wage and value grow somewhat, before the job disappears.

The excess is paid from profits; by reducing expenditure on other employers' costs like maintenance, research and development, new equipment, and buildings; and from private and government borrowings—borrowing from the future to try to prop up present consumption levels.

The amount of monetary breathing space available in these areas determines how far and for how long the wage can exceed the value of a job before it must cease to be available. Companies that are cut to the minimum bearable margin between revenue and outlays have no room to employ anyone extra if that person's wage must exceed the value of the work they do.

The case of government employment is different, because of a difference of aims.

Private companies must have as their primary aim to make money for their owners and shareholders, with the structuring of particular goods and services a means to an end. By contrast, the prime aim of government departments is to perform particular functions which are seen to be necessary and unlikely to be performed otherwise. To do this it is necessary to spend whatever money it takes, up to the limits imposed by competing needs and by the revenue it is possible to raise or borrow.

Thus it is in the public sector we find the highest proportion of workers who are paid more than the value of their work. In this case the excess is made up at the expense of profits, wages, maintenance and investment in the private sector, and of future consumption. But the burden is spread over the whole economy, and the workers cannot be laid off by any private employer. The government controls their employment according to different criteria from those in the private sector.

Transfer payments, pensions, benefits, and allowances are money paid in exchange for no work at all. This is necessary for those who cannot work to be able to live independently. Allowance must always be made for such payments.

Fight Unemployment or Inflation First?

Public sector employment and transfer payments are limited by the amount of revenue which can be raised, which in turn is limited by how much the private sector can provide without ceasing to be viable, or how much can be borrowed without creating a "deficit bomb" as in the U.S.A.

To achieve full employment it is necessary to give this goal priority over all others. However the "price to be paid for full employment" must not have an effect contrary to its purpose, so that society ends up paying a price without receiving the goods.

Depending on their colour, politicians make a false choice between fighting unemployment first, or giving priority to lowering inflation. It is currently believed that full employment can only be achieved at the cost of higher inflation and deficits and that holding inflation down must be at the cost of high unemployment.

This fallacy arises from incomplete understanding of Keynes' theory and, as mentioned earlier, a mistaken belief that his remedies for the economic problems of his time are appropriate for any economic ailment that displays unemployment as a symptom.

Under modern conditions, the increased inflation is a sign that the remedies for the 1930s are not appropriate today. The deficit financing involved and the inflation this helps to cause exert downward pressure on throughput; the latter because it causes uncertainty and reduces the marginal efficiency of capital, and both because they increase interest rates. The effect is upward pressure on unemployment.

Of course, policies currently pursued either to reduce unemployment or control inflation, tend to succeed, if at all, with one at the expense of the other. But this is not because full employment and low inflation are incompatible; it is because the policies worsen the underlying problem of ratio distortion, aggravating its effects and producing a rise in inflation out of proportion to the fall in unemployment, or vice versa, depending on which one is being attacked first.

A sustained attack on inflation brings it down somewhat at the cost of a larger proportionate rise in unemployment.

The latter causes a change in government policy or in government itself, and an attack on unemployment begins, which may reduce it somewhat at the cost of a disproportionate rise in inflation.

This is why every swing of "boom" and "recession" in recent years has, over the full cycle, left the combined problem of unemployment and inflation at a higher level than before.

The reality is that modern inflation, high public debt, and unemployment in the more perfluent nations are symptoms of the one problem, rather than separate problems between which we must choose. As an analogy, a doctor treating a patient should not make a choice to treat one symptom to the neglect or worsening of another. Rather the underlying disease, which gives rise to both symptoms, should be attacked.

The problem has been stated, and will be summarised again; external constraints slow down the rate of throughput increase; excessive expectations push up money wages; this pushes up unemployment, inflation, and deficits; all four upward pressures depress throughput and current remedies for them worsen them and depress throughput further, pushing up unemployment and still creating upward pressure on wages.

The seed of the problem: indefinitely increasing throughput depleting limited resources, and wage demands based on what people think they ought to be able to buy rather than on what the economy can make available at any time.

Earlier it was said that rising or maintained material living standards cannot forever go together with full employment. In the light of what has been said here, a general statement can be made.

Full employment (a) and moderate inflation (b) and moderate interest rates (c) can always exist together; b and c and the maintenance of living standards for those employed (d) can always exist together.

But a, b, c and d cannot always exist together. They can do so for short periods, but this happy state is not sustainable.

Digression: Work and Jobs

The Mitterand socialist government in France hoped to create tens of thousands of jobs by cutting working hours. The basic working week was to carry the same pay, therefore each hour worked was to carry more pay. The work not done as a result of the reduction of hours per worker was supposed to require the engagement of extra hands to get it done.

The mistaken assumption behind this policy was that the amount of work available in an economy at any time is fixed like the amount of fresh water available; and that to take up the unemployed it is necessary only (i) to reduce the amount of work for each worker, to share it around, rather as reducing the amount of water consumed by each person would make water available to those with none; or (ii) to start new projects, to create a greater amount of work, analogous to increasing the water supply to make water available to those with none, without reducing the water consumption of people currently being supplied.

Related to this assumption is the false one that social ideals can be pursued by raising wages without affecting the number of jobs available.

Certainly the amount of wealth throughputting activity in the economy is one determinant of the number of jobs that the economy can support. But another important determinant is the size of wages paid; not only in the aggregate but in the levels paid to particular occupations.

This determinant operates both directly through its effect on the profitability of hiring workers, and indirectly through its effect on the level of economic activity or the incentive to mechanise and automate the structuring of goods and services.

So the number of jobs possible in an economy at any time is not fixed like the water supply. There can be enough jobs for every worker, or for only a fraction of the willing and able work force, depending on three main sets of variables: the throughput rate, the proportion of the money supply flowing through the wages channel, and the relationship of the wage paid for a particular line of work to the market price of the goods and services made available through the practice of that line of work.

The practical result of the Mitterand government's policy of trying to create more jobs by cutting working hours was that jobs were actually eliminated. The work that could have been done at a lower wage continued undone, and some work being done at existing wages disappeared or became more mechanised as hourly labour costs rose.

This was another example of a policy producing an effect opposite to that intended, due to errors in the assumptions on which the policy was based.

Finally, it might be noted that instead of having to start new projects to create jobs, it is really a case of creating jobs (by cutting wage costs) to enable new projects to be started. People start new economic activities not primarily to employ people, but to make money.

Other "Job Creation" Schemes

The statements in this chapter apply particularly to the modern economic predicament and do not necessarily hold true for every form of economic malaise; for instance, they would have been inaccurate for the Great Depression of the 1930s.

In another recent response to unemployment, money is provided to employ people by government borrowing or printing additional money to provide, for extra people, money wages at existing wage levels.

The borrowing puts more pressure on the depleted supply of loanable funds; the printing causes aggregate income to rise faster than net throughput, increasing the inflation rate. Both measures worsen ratio distortion in favour of the aggregate income channel.

Consequent on this there is downward pressure on throughput and upward pressure on money prices. So real wages fall leading to upward pressure on money wages, which worsens its cause and acts against any reduction in unemployment initially achieved.

Another scheme is to provide subsidies to lower the price and increase sales of goods in hopes of maintaining or increasing employment in making the goods. This is, in a different guise, effectively the same as the previous scheme; money is borrowed or printed to maintain money wages at a level and for a proportion of the work force that could not otherwise be achieved. Its achievement is shortlived because the consequences are the same as in the case of direct temporary job creation through increasing the money supply on the side of wages, that is, increasing the proportion of money flowing through the wages channel. The subsidy policy works against its own purpose.

A nation practising these schemes is, of course, disadvantaged in trade with countries not doing so. This makes a further contribution to the job-eliminating, counter-intentional effects of these schemes in the countries which practice them, though there may be a gain of jobs in other countries so the human race as a whole is not necessarily disadvantaged, which is what matters.

Schemes more likely actually to create jobs would entail holding the proportion of money flowing through the wages channel constant, and sharing the money round more workers by reducing money wages. This has been set forth elsewhere, as has the more practical idea of letting the proportion of money flowing through the wages channel fall by freezing money wages and allowing the natural rise in money quantity to reduce that proportion.

The theory behind the current schemes is that if greatly increased money is paid to the unemployed, either for doing nothing or engaging in activity that in itself contributes nothing to the flow of goods and services in the economy (as J. M. Keynes suggested, setting the unemployed to work digging up money buried in disused mines), then the extra money in people's pockets will contribute so much extra to consumer demand as to stimulate enough additional structuring of goods and services to maintain the purchasing power of those working and employ all those not working at comparable real wages.

This argument has been discussed in other chapters. The theory was valid for the Great Depression, but the problems of today are different.

Digression: Renewal and Recycling of Resources; Wages and Jobs

It is possible for some time to consume a resource faster than its renewal rate, just as a business can for some time consume its accumulated money capital faster than it takes money in (this is only an illustration and does not confuse money with wealth). But for the business to survive and go on providing jobs, it must lay money out no faster than the money comes in.

Accurate data are available on the quantity, depletion rate, and natural renewal rate of many resources. This availability can be expected to improve in accuracy and completeness in the future.

The rate of depletion of resource after resource must be

brought below its renewal rate. Apart from, obviously, reducing the consumption rate, the renewal rate can be increased to some extent for many resources, for example, aluminum.

The mining of bauxite, its processing into aluminum, and subsequent wide dispersal into the environment would lead to very low availability of the aluminum resource, because one determinant of availability is concentration, which also determines the difference between gross and net throughput for a resource. The natural rate of reconcentration of the highly dispersed metal into convenient thick layers of bauxite ore is very low, if it exists.

The renewal rate can be usefully increased by deliberate human efforts to collect every scrap of used metal for restructuring into fresh metal products. One looks forward to a future time when such a process would be part and parcel of the economic system, an inescapable accompaniment to the use of the metal; but in our present relatively primitive economic state it is resisted, practiced only to a marginal extent, and regarded as a "cost" that it is not "economic" to bear.

Recycling of aluminum, of other metals, and also of materials such as paper, cloth, glass, or building material would provide employment and reduce resource throughput by reducing the need to extract raw materials to make totally fresh supplies—two important economic benefits.

But nowhere near as much recycling is done as could be, because in many cases not enough money can be got for the renewed materials to pay the wages of the necessary workers.

So in this example, excessive wages not only prevent employment but undermine the economy by causing the accelerated depletion of the resource base.

Of course it is necessary for the money outlay required for the process of reconcentrating metals to be no greater than the money price obtained for them when they are ready for sale to manufacturers. But the reconcentration is a form of economic growth since it increases renewal rate and reduces the depletion rate; thus it must not be abandoned because the money balance is unfavourable. Rather the process must be continued and expanded, and the money situation must be coerced into conformity with this primary objective.

Putting it another way, recycling or reconcentrating are currently described as "uneconomic" in those cases where money outlay would be greater than money income, simply because of that. In fact, according to better developed criteria consistent with the ideas in this book, recycling, by creating jobs and reducing the need for resource throughput, would be economic just because of those effects. An uneconomic project would be one that depleted or accelerated depletion of the resource base, which means destroying jobs and reducing living standards.

It follows that wages in renewal rate boosting industries (RRBI) must not be determined, as now, by arbitrary and often unrealistic ideas about the spending power to which workers have a right. Such ideas in practice often defeat their goal by eroding the purchasing power of money or eliminating jobs. It is no comfort to a worker to know that his job would be well paid if he had it when no one can afford to employ him at that rate of pay.

Instead, RRBI, being "economic" in themselves, quite independently of the state of wage levels, must be kept going and this must be the overriding priority to which wage levels must submit and by which they must be limited, given the state of labour-saving technology at any time.

The limitation on wages is stricter in the case of RRBI than in the case of throughput rate boosting industries.

If a project is economic according to the better developed criteria outlined above, then it must go forward. If the money balance is unfavourable then the money aspect of the project must be manipulated to obtain a favourable balance. There are several ways of doing this.

Wages for workers could be cut, which is possible by abolishing the minimum wage, restructuring unemployment payments (these would be useful measures in general), and weakening trade unions in the relevant area.

Improved technology requiring less paid labour input per unit of recycled material can be developed; this would require money investment that could take a while to recoup.

A recycling business could be government subsidised so that recycled material could be sold at attractive prices, or new resource extraction could be taxed so that the full price of recycled material would still be attractive in comparison with material made from newly extracted resources. The latter option would be better because the government would be dampening consumption while at the same time not piling up debt, rather reducing it. The workers losing their jobs in resource extraction industries as a result could be taken up by recycling industries.

Ratio Distortion and Consumption

Before and during the Great Depression there was under-consumption due to chronic underpayment of workers—fewer goods and services were being consumed than available workers and plants could structure. But what of today, when chronic overpayment of workers is the distortion affecting more perfluent economies?

Obviously there cannot be "overconsumption" as a sim-ple contrast to underconsumption. Goods and services can be sold more slowly than they can be made, leading to a pile up of unsold goods, losses by manufacturers, reduced manufacture, thus job losses. But goods and services cannot be consumed faster than they are made available.

So what happens?

The depressing effect on economic activity caused by too much money flowing through the wages channel begins with its effect on prices.

Upward pressure on prices results from profits being too low, wages being too high a fraction of outlays, interest rates being high on borrowings that are too high a fraction of income and drawing on too low a capital pool, and demand pull from consumers. More will be said a few paragraphs hence on that point.

The resulting excessive rate of price increases reduces the marginal efficiency of capital, causing companies to withhold investment that might employ people directly or subsequently.

Apart from that the investment could be in some scheme, such as developing renewable or alternative energy sources, solar, biomass, oil shale, which would relieve the pressure on limited, nonrenewable oil; or in new equipment to structure the same quantity of goods from less resources, thus retarding the progress of resource depletion and of value inflation.

The high price increase rate also aggravates its causes by boosting interest rates and increasing pressure for wage rises.

If the Keynesian term "underconsumption" is changed to "inadequate demand," then the opposite "excessive demand" makes more practical sense than "overconsumption" as a description of the case at the present time.

The term consumer demand is equivalent to the proportionate flow of money through the wages, transfer payments, and consumer debt channels. Aggregate demand is not the same and will be discussed in the next chapter.

Referring to an earlier chapter, "The Throughput Chain," we can picture the demand link being smaller than the "production" (goods and services structuring) link in the 1920s and 1930s, but larger than it in our own time. In the former case, the effect was to depress prices and the rate of structuring, making it less than was possible given the existing work force, plant, and resource availability. In the latter case, in our own time, the effect is not to increase the rate of structuring of goods and services above what is allowed by the existing work force, plant, and resource availability, since that would be impossible; rather, the effect is worked out entirely in pushing up prices.

Keynes foresaw that if consumer demand went on increasing after full employment had been reached, true inflation, a decrease in the value of money, would result. This has come true and persisting over many years has caused unemployment to rise again. But this is not of the same kind that can be banished by further increases in consumer demand, since this is what caused it in the first place. Rather, consumer demand has an achievable optimum relative level (but see the next chapter, "Aggregate Demand—Components and Internal Ratio"). This is just repeating an earlier point in different terms. So job creation schemes based on boosting consumer demand may, under current conditions, become job destruction schemes. This will be discussed further in the chapter "Full Wage Indexation—Kindergarten Economics."

Aggregate Demand—Components and Internal Ratio

Before going any further it is necessary to discuss the term aggregate demand.

Aggregate demand is the sum of two components—investment spending and consumer spending. It would be better if these were treated separately as independent channels through which money flows, since the relation between them is by no means constant in the sense that they can be lumped together and boosted or damped down together.

During the Great Depression, investment and consumer spending power were both very depressed. At other times, investment was high with wages low, so that aggregate demand was adequate. In our own time, consumer demand is too high but investment spending too low, so that aggregate demand may appear to be at least not badly depressed. But the internal ratio of aggregate demand, between consumer and investment demand, is crucial in determining the effect of the level of aggregate demand on economic activity, employment, and the rate of price increases.

Investment is depressed because (apart from disincentives) too little money capital is being accumulated; this is caused by the flow of money through the profits and savings channel being relatively too small. This widens the margin by which interest rates must always exceed the price increase rate. Interest rates are the mechanism whereby borrowing demand is matched to the amount of money available for borrowing.

There are several effects of this.

Depreciation of plant and equipment is not being made good fast enough. Capital goods are not being improved, and technology is not developing as fast as might be. This is true

107

even of go-go areas like microelectronics.

Also, the ever widening difference between gross and net throughput resulting from steady wealth depletion requires that the proportion of money flowing into capital accumulation for investment must steadily rise, not fall. This increasing flow would be felt as value inflation as discussed earlier.

During the Great Depression, money capital was plentiful but demand for it was low because wages were too low to provide enough consumer demand to stimulate enough investment to employ the money capital (this implies, correctly, that the two components of aggregate demand are determinants, though not the sole determinants, of each other).

Today, wages are too high and money that should be accumulating as loanable funds is going into the consumer demand channel. This implies two other possible methods of regaining full employment by adjusting the proportionate flows of money, apart from the already mentioned one of cutting wages.

One is to turn the Keynesian Great Depression remedy on its head. Instead of putting more money into consumers' pockets, transfer money to companies to increase their profits and stimulate investment.

This could not be done by borrowing idle capital, since this is not plentiful as in the depression. Money would need to be printed, deliberately created by the monetary authority, and added to the capital pool for borrowing or given to companies to pad profit margins.

The contrived nature of this arrangement could encourage waste and inefficiency in business, and the required large increase in the money supply could be inflationary by being greater than any increase in economic activity that it might stimulate. The inflation would then discourage investment.

A Wage Freeze

Another way, more practical and even already tried though without sufficient firmness or persistence, is to freeze money wages and salaries indefinitely and allow normal increases in the money supply to force more and more into other channels—profits and investment capital.

This would also have the effect of putting upward pressure on money prices and downward pressure on real wages. Thus wages would steadily decrease as a fraction of the outlay needed to make goods and services, so that in more and more cases it would become worthwhile financially to employ people previously excluded from the work force.

The point to keep in mind is that in the private sector, if it is profitable to employ people, they will be employed; if not, they won't.

Once the prolonged freeze had achieved full employment, which it would eventually in the absence of severe economic disruption, a new wage adjustment system, as described in the next chapter but one, could be instituted.

Full Wage Indexation—Kindergarten Economics

Full Wage Indexation (FWI), indexing wages to the full Consumer Price Index, that is, increasing money wages at regular intervals by the same proportion as the rate of price increases during those intervals, is intended to maintain living standards by maintaining real wages. This is kindergarten economics.

The idea is that if prices go up by say, 10 percent over

109

three months, through whatever cause, then if you increase money wages by 10 percent at the end of the three months, purchasing power, real wages, will be restored to what they were at the start of the three months.

In fact real wages are not the same as money wages; purchasing power is not a simple function of money wages. It is a function of throughput, population, and the distribution of money income.

In turn, one determinant of throughput is, as already stated, the relative proportions of money flowing through different channels in the economy.

The rate of change of prices is erroneously called inflation. It includes inflation but it is not the same thing. It is the resultant of several rates of change (each of which have one or more different determinants, including each other). These are: (i) value inflation (defined earlier); and rates of change of (ii) taxes, (iii) wages, (iv) interest rates, (v) and currency exchange rates; (vi) the rate of improvement of technology and (vii), obviously, the rate of change of money value, this being determined by the difference between the rates of change of the money supply and of the level of economic activity.

The more cumbersome but more precise term "rate of change" is used throughout the previous paragraph rather than "increase" because although the rates of change are usually upward, this does not have to be so and has not always been so.

The expectations and business decisions, rational or otherwise, of those responsible for setting prices affect the variables listed above, and in turn are affected by them.

The combined effect of the variables fluctuates over time. The relevant point for us today is that since the early 1970s, prices have risen faster than throughput.

Indexing wages to the full CPI, forcing them to rise as fast as prices, causes wages to rise faster than throughput.

110

This causes a steadily worsening ratio distortion.

This affects all the rates of change listed earlier in the direction of increasing the upward rate of change of prices that in turn increases the upward rate of change of money wages.

The rate of devaluation of money will rise. Interest rates will rise because of this and because borrowing demand would rise for three reasons: (i) governments would borrow more to pay escalating public sector wages and more and higher welfare transfers, (ii) consumers would borrow more because of the greater confidence engendered by regular money wage increases, and (iii) many companies would buy time in the face of insufficient profits by borrowing more.

The currency of the country with a FWI policy tends to fall in value relative to currencies of countries without FWI.

The effect of improving technology on retarding the rate of increase of prices of goods and services is lessened because the rate of improvement of technology, determined in part by the availability of investment and development finance, is slowed by insufficient profits and higher interest rates. As a counter to this, insufficient profits and ever-rising money wages provide a greater incentive than before to improve technology to achieve higher productivity, that is to reduce the work force needed for a particular rate of structuring of goods and services.

All these effects apply to the modern context in which the end result of a policy of FWI is not to maintain real wages, but actually to reduce them. That is, the net result of each upward adjustment in money wages is to reduce real wages, not only relative to what they were before the adjustment, but relative to what they would have been had no upward adjustment taken place.

So the effect of a policy of FWI is quite opposite to the intention.

A Better Wage-fixing System

The money wage freeze referred to earlier, if maintained long enough to bring wages at the lower levels in line with the money value of the work for which the wages are paid, would lead to many workers at higher wage and salary levels being underpaid since lower level remuneration has risen disproportionately in recent years. This underpayment would need adjustment separately from the universal wage-fixing system about to be described.

A preliminary point is that wage fixing must be taken away from the arena of conflict among stronger and weaker unions, stronger and weaker companies, and political ideology and vote-catching. High unemployment is such a serious social blight (as Keynes knew, but too many people today seem not to recognise) that wage fixing should not be left to the vagaries of human nature but must be the sole province of an independent objective authority assisted by computers and given strong legal power to obtain any and all statistics relevant to its work.

It is unlikely that, over time, the wage fraction of total money flow can be maintained at exactly the right size, or that unemployment can stay always at a practical minimum, that is no involuntary unemployment. The best that can be realised is that the wage fraction can remain roughly, a little more or less, at the optimum, and that involuntary unemployment can stay negligible. It is certainly possible to avoid the gross ratio distortions and excessive unemployment experienced during the twentieth century.

Once unemployment has fallen to near practical minimum, a money wage indexation should be instituted, not to maintain living standards, but to maintain full or near-full employment during all economic ups and downs.

To repeat the contrast between what is proposed and what is currently practiced, instead of giving priority to trying to maintain living standards and letting the unemployment level go up and down as now, it is proposed that maintaining full employment should be the primary goal and living standards should be allowed to fluctuate as economic conditions dictate. Whatever is available would then be more justly shared, and the economy, being freed from other stresses associated with ratio distortion, would be in near best shape to take best advantage of whatever wealth parameters it has to accommodate. Those parameters are the availability of wealth and the renewal rate and, therefore, the sustainable throughput rate of each wealth species (i.e., resource).

Of course a wealth species can be throughput faster than its renewal rate, but such throughput is not sustainable.

The effect on inflation and interest rates of maintaining optimum proportions of money flow in the economy will be discussed more fully later.

When the new type of indexation starts, the money wage indexation rate should be determined by three variables:

(i) the rate of throughput increase (TI), erroneously called now the "economic growth rate."

(ii) the rate of increase of the able and willing work force, usable figures on the size of and changes in which are already available.

(iii) the rate of change in the value of money, determined by the relation between two rates of change, of money supply, and throughput.

TI is a component of variables one and three, and so it cancels out, as will be demonstrated shortly. This solves the question that will have arisen: "How do you measure throughput in money units consistent over time?" There is no need in this case.

WORK FORCE in what follows, means those in work plus those actively seeking work, apart from changing jobs. If unemployment is minimal the latter quantity should be small.

At the end of one quarter, let throughput = $T(1)$, money supply = $M(1)$, workforce = $W(1)$.

At the end of the next quarter, let throughput = $T(2)$, money supply = $M(2)$, workforce = $W(2)$.

The value of money (MV) varies directly with throughput, but inversely with the money supply.

So: New MV = old MV $\times$ $M(1)$ $\times$ $T(2)$ / $M(2)$ $\times$ $T(1)$.

Money wages must change inversely as any change in MV, change directly as any TI, and change inversely as any change in workforce.

So, in this example:

New money wage =

$$\text{old money wage} \times \frac{M(2) \times T(1) \times T(2) \times W(1)}{M(1) \times T(2) \times T(1) \times W(2)}$$

= old money wage $\times$ $M(2)$ $\times$ $W(1)$ / $M(1)$ $\times$ $W(2)$.

The TI term, $T(2)$ / $T(1)$, figures inversely in determining the change in money value and directly as one of the three terms determining the required change in money wage. So TI cancels out. Money wages need basically be indexed to just the money supply and the work force.

"Basically," because a valid objection to the simplicity of this scheme is that it is only permanently applicable in an economy where throughput per worker in every occupation always changes at the same rate. Obviously this is not and never has been the case. However the differences in rates of throughput change should be small enough for the approxi-

114

mation to suffice over short periods. Its simplicity is an advantage which outweighs small, not life-threatening injustices which will advantage some and disadvantage others from quarter to quarter.

But there must be provision for cases where, in a particular occupation, throughput per worker changes at a rate different from the aggregate, the change being in one direction for so many quarters in a row that an excessively wide gap opens up between what the workers are paid and what their work is worth (there must always be such a gap in the employer's favour anyway).

If this happens there are two possibilities:

If the gap is to the money advantage of the workers affected, their jobs will be reduced through automation or neglect, though the ones left employed will have a spending power advantage at the expense of the rest of the work force.

If the gap yawns the other way, the workers affected will be underpaid. This will tend to increase the security of their jobs but will make their spending power less than it could be and affect the whole economy adversely, because the aggregate spending power of the population will be less than optimum. Remember that this discussion is taking place in a context where near-optimum proportionate money flows have been achieved. If the money value of work rises faster than the wage for that work in one industry, then in that area proportionate flows will be distorted against wages. This distortion will affect the whole economy in ways analogous to, though less severe than, the Great Depression, when ratio distortion of this kind was severe and general.

So special determinations will be necessary from time to time to correct anomalies in particular occupations.

At one time such determinations would have been a daunting task taking much time and expense, handling masses of data, and open to all sorts of errors and suspicion and abuse. But today and in the future we have increasingly pow-

115

erful technology for computation and for the storage and retrieval of information. Once the program is written determination should be a matter of minutes on each occasion and should be able to be error free, quick and objective enough to be respected. An independent authority, similar to the judiciary, should be responsible for the process.

It would not be desirable to make such special adjustments whenever a particular industry showed a drift away from an optimum relationship of wages to work value. It would be better, and feasible, to keep every industry under constant review and wait until the drift had reached a certain extent before making a special adjustment. In fast-changing industries the interval between special adjustments might be short; but it might be years with older, more stable industries. Meanwhile all workers would continue to receive the quarterly money-wage indexation changes described earlier. This would be guaranteed.

When a special upward adjustment is made, where does the money come from?

The adjustment is only required because the money value of the work under review has risen faster than wages, over a period. So the money for the adjustment would come out of profits. The company could increase prices to cover the increased wages, but in doing so would (i) nullify the adjustment, creating grounds for another adjustment and (ii) disadvantage the company in the marketplace. No doubt some companies would meet required upward wage adjustments by increasing prices, but they would learn the hard way that this would set off a self-reinforcing process damaging to the company and to its workers' jobs.

Of course it might happen that the money value of the work under review has actually dropped relative to wages over a period. This is not usual but it is possible. In this case money wages would have to be adjusted downwards. This could lead to strikes the first time it happened. Strikes of that kind would have to be weathered firmly, with no compromise on the basic principles vital to the maintenance of the precious social benefit of full employment.

Employment and the Steady State

It is necessary here to repeat a point made or implied earlier, that the level and rate of change of economic activity and the level of unemployment are to a large extent independent of one another. Not totally independent of course, each is one determinant of the other. But it is possible, depending on whether and to what extent and in what sense ratio distortion exists, to have full employment at a time of falling throughput, or high unemployment at a time of steady or rising throughput.

This denies the current idea that endless economic "growth," i.e., TI, is a sine qua non of full employment, and conversely that the answer to unemployment is always to achieve a higher TI rate no matter by what means or for how short a time.

So advocates of the view that economic activity cannot endlessly increase against limited global resources need not feel that their view condemns ever more millions to unemployment. Full employment can be maintained under a "steady state" economic regime, that is, one where the throughput rate of all resources is no greater than their renewal rate. The human economy would be in dynamic equilibrium with the world environment.

Thus the steady state, as well as being the only way for

the human economy to survive and be healthy in the future, need not be "static" and "growthless" as has been claimed by those who feel threatened by anything new. It would be full of change, and vibrant activity and growth would be available in ways defined earlier on; but it would also be self-sustaining and self-enhancing, instead of self-destructive as is the present system.

As already mentioned it is not possible forever to have rising material living standards and full employment together. They occurred together for a minority of the world's people for a few decades and this was an exceptional piece of luck rather than the norm. The norm is that we have to choose between one and the other, and as a matter of social justice and practical politics we must choose full employment, and hold to that choice no matter what.

Consumer-led Recovery

This chapter will cross at a different angle, ground covered already.

The belief is still currently widespread, and held by persons of influence in economic affairs, that a general increase in wages will boost the economy, i.e., increase the throughput rate and its derivative by increasing consumer demand.

As already discussed, this would apply to modern problems, for which it is quite inappropriate, the solution that was correct for the depression of the 1930s.

In a radio talk in Australia during 1983, the speaker said that the problem of industry and the economy was not the cost of wages, or the cost of finance, the problem was lack of demand. That is, the rate of spending in the economy was too low. Two hundred manufacturers had been asked "What single factor, if any, is most limiting your ability to increase production?" They did not say the cost of labour, the cost of finance, or the availability of materials. Over 90 percent of them said "Lack of Orders." In the previous eighteen months the lack of orders had risen dramatically. It had been declining as a factor until the end of 1981. Since then, the speaker said, lack of orders had been the main problem. He said that the aim of economic policy should be to increase incomes and that meant increasing disposable incomes for the economy as a whole and particularly those that are at present unemployed.

This might be a case of getting a report of a symptom and ascribing it to only one possible cause, as though that cause were the only one. In this case it was the speaker's preference.

"Lack of Orders" in the sense that orders are not sufficient to maintain full employment, would be the immediate cause of unemployment, the overt symptom of economic trouble, no matter what the particular nature of the trouble.

The important question is, what are the original causes of the lack of orders? Lack of orders is not an original cause; it is an effect, which in turn is the cause of subsequent economic effects.

In the Great Depression, lack of orders was in fact caused by insufficient consumer spending because too little money income was flowing into the wages channel. In the current economic malaise, lack of orders is caused by purchasers not being able to afford the prices for all the wholesale consumer goods and producer goods that would need to be structured to maintain full employment.

Once again, this looks similar to the problem in the depression. The difference is that wages are a higher proportion of the price of goods and services than they were in the depression. One might think, all right, prices are boosted by wages, but so is spending power, in the same proportion, so there should be no downward pressure on consumer demand.

But it is not as simple as that. There is a kind of "multiplier effect" here, because the excessive wages boost prices at every stage of the process whereby goods become available for purchase. This process entails the extraction of wealth, the development and construction of industrial plants, the structuring of wealth into goods, transport to shops, and sale to consumers.

So one consumer only has one excessive margin of money wages to spend, but must pay prices boosted by more than one excessive wage margin.

Thus ratio distortion in the direction of too much money flowing into the wages channel exerts downward pressure on spending power.

One may ask, doesn't this type of multiplier effect work in the other direction when wages are too small a fraction of money flow? Doesn't the wage deficiency at every stage depress prices by several deficiencies, making goods easier to buy for each consumer suffering only one deficiency, thus boosting purchasing power?

The mistaken assumption behind this question would be that the effect of wages on prices is linear. The relationship of wages to prices is not linear. The boost to prices resulting from, say, a 10 percent excess of money flowing in the wages channel (though it would be virtually impossible to measure the actual amount of excess or deficiency) would be greater than the depression of prices resulting from a comparable deficiency of money flowing in the wages channel.

The Slave Economy

To back up this statement, consider the case of an economy where there are no wages—where all the extraction of wealth, structuring and selling of goods and services is done by slave labour. Actually this is a fair approximation to the economy of the slave-owning states of North America, briefly the Confederate States of America, during the last century.

In such an economy goods and services still are made, still cost something to make available, still have a price, and are still consumed. But there is no consumer demand as we would understand it within a slave economy; the vast majority of the population cannot demand anything, make market choices, have consumer goals, or accumulate capital as savings. They get what they are given, which is little more than the bare minimum needed to keep them alive and working.

Such consumer demand as there is comes from the owners of the slaves and the wealth and the means of its transformation into goods. This demand is small and limited in range. The main money flow through the economy comes from other economies outside who purchase the goods, mainly primary produce, made by the slaves. Since the local market for most goods and services is too small to support local secondary and tertiary industries, these also are located in other economies. Local industries are mainly primary industries.

Full employment cannot be guaranteed because although labour has no money price, it still has a price in the limited subsistence goods required by the slave. With only a few large, basic local industries and all employment under the control of a few, there is no guarantee of enough work to justify feeding all the slaves, and no mechanism to adjust the economy to a state of full employment since there are no wages to manipulate.

The main reason the Confederate States of America lost the 1861–65 Civil War was that, being virtually isolated by blockades and sanctions, their economy could not provide for a long war effort against the industrial, diversified economy of the "Yankees." Modern wars are won by superior

121

economies rather than by greater generals.

It was said at the start of that civil war that the CSA could win if they did it quickly, but they would be sure to lose a war which lasted longer than a year.

So to reiterate a point made earlier; wages must exist, they must not be too low, but they cannot go on increasing indefinitely without damage to economic activity and employment. There is an optimum proportion of wages to total money flow that cannot be determined theoretically in any situation, but is only achieved by practical freeze or boost measures taken after examination of the symptoms of distress shown by the economy, followed by correct diagnosis of the sense in which ratio distortion exists—towards wages or the other way.

Interest Rates and Ratio Distortion

It is necessary for a lender of money to charge interest because the purchasing power of each money unit is generally expected to fall with time. This has been the trend historically and the very operation of an economy tends to make it so.

So, in order for the lender to show a profit in terms of purchasing power on the transaction they must charge interest equal to the rate of price increases (comprising inflation plus other influences) plus a profit margin.

Lenders, like everyone else, want an ever-rising living standard, so the interest rate they charge must be sufficient to show a purchasing power profit.

However this consideration must be balanced with the need to attract borrowers. If the interest rate is so high, that the purchasing power a borrower has to lose in interest charges is expected to be greater than the purchasing power they will gain in the end by borrowing the money, then they won't borrow.

So interest rates appear to be determined by the tussle between lenders and borrowers for the best purchasing power advantage. But there are three points to note.

(i) Interest rates must be regulated to some degree, otherwise too much rapid unpredictable movement and large variations would create too much uncertainty.

(ii) A borrower often needs money for a particular purpose which cannot be postponed or abandoned. In this situation they must borrow money at a particular time even if the interest rate is so high that they expect a net loss of purchasing power in the longer term.

(iii) An important determinant of interest rates is the supply-demand one; the relation between the supply of money available for lending and the demand for loans from government, business, and consumers.

Upward pressure on interest rates results if demand exceeds supply, and downward pressure if supply exceeds demand.

Since about 1970, in the more perfluent nations demand for loans has increased faster than the supply of loanable funds. This has put upward pressure on interest rates.

Wealth depletion has caused value inflation (see chapter "Value Inflation—the Trigger, Not the Bullet") to appear as a component of price increases. Because of the pressure of high and rising expectations taking no account of resource limits, this value inflation has triggered further price increases.

Wealth depletion also puts downward pressure on net throughput, not necessarily reducing it, but causing it to rise more slowly than expected.

Ratio distortion in the direction of wages has developed and an excessive rate of price increases has become chronic, with occasional remission.

The combination of a high price increase rate with the upward pressure resulting from supply-demand forces produces chronically high interest rates which are a reliable symptom of ratio distortion in the wage direction.

Demographic Trends and Living Standards

People are agents of throughput and the younger, healthier, and less resistant to change are the people (for a given population, state of technology, and resource availability), then the larger and better quality the throughput they can achieve.

In more perfluent countries, in recent years, several factors have combined to effect a steady increase in the average age of the population.

There was an unusually high birthrate between 1946 and 1952. There has been a generally falling birthrate since then.

Medical and nutrition improvements have increased people's life expectancy.

The effect of this increase in the median age of populations will increasingly be to depress the throughput rate. At the same time, pensions and other benefits will demand an ever-increasing proportion of money flow in the economy.

The aging populations will achieve a lower rate of throughput increase than the same circumstances would have allowed more vigorous populations, and material living standard expectations will be further ahead of reality. The latter point will be aggravated by the fact that, even with the median age of the populations in the most perfluent nations staying the same, the expectations of today's young people on retirement will be much higher than those of the present crop of old people; and the pressure from the pensioner lobby for higher payments will be greater from this factor alone, apart from the greater number, vigour, and longevity of the old, and their probable earlier retirement. Today Gran might be happy to get a bus to go in to the shops but today's young people, the future's pensioners, will expect to roar everywhere in a large powerful car even when they are no longer contributing their work to society.

The demand for transfer payments to pensioners will increase faster than the rate of increase of those requiring pensions, because the living standard expectations of each successive retiring group will be higher.

While throughput per person is falling or rising more slowly, the proportion of the population causing that throughput is falling and everyone's expectations are rising, there are ever fewer workers supporting each pensioner and carrying each aging, less efficient worker.

There are three ways of supporting this ever-growing burden of transfer payments. Taxes on workers can go on increasing, government debt must increase, or money must be printed to pay pensions.

The first option will grow ever more intolerable and cause rage and conflict between old and young; it will also make working for a living increasingly unattractive, encouraging ever more people to find a way of getting a pension, and exacerbating the problem of an ever-growing burden of transfer payments.

The second procedure amounts to borrowing from the future to pay for present consumption. This might be all right if there were a good chance of repaying the debt, but what chance would there be of that in this case, considering the purpose for which the debt would be incurred? Such borrowing would put upward pressure on interest rates. Also, since consumption per person is a function of the availability of goods and services and the distribution of personal money income, not simply of the number of currency units a person has, it will cause inflation by making each currency unit able to command fewer goods and services.

That last point applies more directly to the measure of simply printing money. The consequences of an increase in the inflation rate have been looked at in other chapters.

The rate of technology improvement is slowed by the aging of the population. This also works against maintaining or increasing throughput.

One advantage, a large one, of this whole development is that the rate of depletion of wealth is slowed, buying more time for economic reform and depriving the less perfluent nations of less throughput, that is allowing them more throughput than they might otherwise have had.

This advantage is enhanced by the fact that the more perfluent populations are smaller than they could have been and are growing more slowly.

This discussion will be resumed after the following digression.

Digression: Bad Economics Good for Conservation?

This digression takes another journey over ground traversed in the chapter "Digression—Resource Consumption, Jobs, and 'Hands Off' " and in the *Foreword*.

In the foregoing discussion of pensions there appears to be a contradiction—the current trend of pension payments threatens severe economic dislocation, but such dislocation slows throughput and conserves wealth. This conflict is general—anything which dislocates economies conserves wealth by slowing throughput or locally halting it. This unfortunately includes war and terrorism. The destruction caused by these is mainly to throughput facilities rather than to the wealth base. This should not be taken as an argument in favour of the evil, destructive side of human activity, rather as a way of pointing up the conflict between present economic systems and the earth's well-being, on which those very economic systems depend.

How may this conflict be resolved?

Not by running economic systems so inefficient that they will never be able either to deplete the wealth base or serve the human race properly; rather by achieving the greatest and best throughput with the fairest distribution permitted by the global environment of the economic organism. The limitations of this environment must be taken into account in practical policies thoroughly interwoven with general economic practice. This is discussed in other parts of this book.

Coping with Aging Populations

An answer must be found to the problems of aging populations in more perfluent countries.

It has been suggested that efforts should be made to achieve and sustain a higher birthrate in the more perfluent countries, to lower the median age and create more taxable workers and more throughput to support ever rising pension demands.

Once the larger generations began to mature, it could be expected that more per person, and better, throughput would follow for a given state of resource availability. But the higher rate of population growth and higher throughput per person would accelerate the decrease of resource availability and thus drag throughput down anyway. The larger, younger population increasing at a higher rate could end up with lower material living standards at the same point in time than would be available to the smaller, older population living with a less efficient economic system and a heavier proportionate pension burden.

The expectations of the younger, bigger population would presumably be rising all the time, because if it were not possible to control the expectations of the growing pensioner lobby, it would not be possible to curb those of the rest of the people.

The vital point here is the limitations on wealth and its (mathematical) derivatives previously discussed. On a flat earth of unlimited resources, there need be no limit to population growth but it also wouldn't matter if all the population were geriatric and, as previously pointed out, there would be no need for any economic system or any doling out of set amounts of buying power.

Besides, the lower birthrate is a result of deliberate choice; people in more perfluent nations are not making love any less than formerly, but given the increasing availability and efficacy of birth control technology in recent times, people are choosing smaller families, partly as a result of the drive for ever higher living standards. As well as being tiring and restrictive, large families act against couples' living standards. It would probably be more difficult to coerce people in perfluent countries to increase the birthrate than it is to persuade people in less perfluent or more crowded places to reduce their family size. This topic is discussed further in the next chapter.

A better idea would be to let the "bulge" of aging people work its way through and gradually disappear, with a population smaller than it would have been, and with a better age distribution and balance coming up behind. This will take decades during which time social stresses will need to be endured.

Expectations will need to be reduced. People will have to be told forcefully and repeatedly, using the same manipulative advertising techniques as have told them the opposite for so long, that material living standards and population cannot forever rise and, in more perfluent nations, the former must fall and the latter level off to give the world economy any hope of becoming fair and sustainable. This point was discussed earlier.

Government payments to the old in some countries have been rising faster per person than wages because of a policy of indexing pensions to the full CPI—a policy not so often applied to wages. Thus purchasing power for pensioners has been rising faster or falling more slowly than for the working population. This might be justified for a while in a situation where pensioners are too badly off compared with wage earners, but it clearly cannot continue indefinitely.

If old age pensions were indexed to gross wages instead of to prices, this would keep the relative spending power of pensioners and workers in step as long as the median age of the population, the life expectancy, and the retiring age remained constant. However, if, as in recent years, the first two of those variables were rising and the last falling, pensioners would still increase their buying power faster or lose it more slowly than workers because ever more taxes or other contributions would need to be raised to pay pensions to the steadily rising proportion of the population eligible for these.

Should pensions instead be indexed to net wages, i.e., after tax? This is complicated on the face of it because net wages are a function of tax levels, which in turn are a function of pension requirements. So pensions would be indexed to a rate of change whose size their setting affects. However it need not be difficult in practice.

Starting at a particular date when pensions were deemed by both recipients and contributors to be at least tolerable, it need only be necessary to declare that thenceforth pensions will rise quarterly by the actual percentage rise in average take-home wages for that quarter.

If there are ever more pensioners then ever more taxes will need to be raised to support them. So take-home pay will rise ever more slowly and may even fall, taking pensions with it.

If money wages were already indexed as described in an earlier section in such a way as to maintain full employment regardless of the effect on living standards, then the whole economy would be ready for adjustment to the quantity and renewal rate limits of the world's resources.

The living standard achievable under this full employment regime will of course become lower as the human population becomes higher. As pointed out repeatedly, no economic plan for the world can work unless human population growth stops. This task, while vital, is more difficult than the objective indexation measures described here and in the section on wage fixing. However it must be achieved and need not be impossible, if certain assumptions and attitudes are challenged.

Stabilising the Human Population

Most people love their children, and children generally are a source of pleasure. Some people even claim to derive deep satisfaction from a houseful of seven or eight youngsters. But it is true to say of most people regardless of race or location that, if they had a really free choice, they would rather have a manageable number—enough for pleasure and company—but not the heavy load of six to a dozen or more.

This is proven by the fact that couples in more perfluent nations, having in recent decades for the first time in history a large measure of choice and control in the matter of child-bearing, are mostly choosing to have just one, two or three, then stop.

Why then do people in the rest of the world have so many babies?

First, it is important to realise that there is not a lot of purposefulness in it—it just happens is the main reason for it. Contraceptives are not as cheap and available as in more perfluent countries. Also, in these countries, most people's lives are what more fortunate world citizens would regard as hard, uncomfortable, insecure, and monotonous. Frequent marital relations may be very important to make life bearable.

It is often said that the higher birthrate in these countries arises from the desire of people to have security for their old age in the form of grown-up offspring to support and care for them. It is more likely that this is a rationalisation, a perceived compensation for the burden of a large family, rather than the purpose for which the childbearing is undertaken. Rather than husband and wife saying "Let's have seven children so we can be provided for in our old age," it is more likely that they say "Well, we've got seven children, we may have more, and it's hard, but at least some of them might help us in our old age."

If they had a free choice, as would be provided by cheap and readily available contraception and national pension and health schemes for those too old to work, then most people in less perfluent countries would prefer to have fewer children, enjoy them more, and not find them such a burden.

It is not quite as simple as that of course—religion is a powerful force opposing contraception in many parts of the world. Religion generally has the effect of opposing anything constructive for reasons that will be discussed in another chapter.

It might be said that contraception and social services are an "internal matter" for nations and that citizens of other nations have no right to intervene. Any economic or social injustice suffered by people anywhere in the world is the rightful concern of people anywhere else in the world. We must all come to regard ourselves as world citizens and artificial borders between peoples must not be allowed to maintain inequalities of rights, opportunities, and economic well-being. Such borders must be regarded as a temporary stage which must be overcome by any means. People must realise that they have a permanent right to intervene in the affairs of other nations if any wrong appears to need righting. This may not always achieve much, but the net effect will help human progress if it contributes to the process of weakening and ultimately dissolving national borders.

"Costs"—What Really Costs Us and What Doesn't?

A new definition of costs is also required. The term at present is muddled and confused in general usage.

Wealth Loss versus Throughput Reduction

Any outlay of money in a national economy is regarded as a "cost" to the nation in the sense of some loss of wealth. This can lead to the absurd idea that if a larger amount of money changes hands when some environmental protection

132

measure is put into effect than would do so if it were not put into effect, then greater economic benefit and wealth can result from not undertaking the measure. This misconception is illustrated first in an article on acid rain and emission controls in a scientific journal in 1984, where it was said that proven damage estimates [from NOx and SOx emissions] were in the millions of dollars per year, while present control costs were in the billions or tighter controls would cost further billions.

This statement was made in support of the argument that measures to reduce or prevent the emission of oxides of sulphur and nitrogen, from fossil fuel power stations, industry and vehicles, would be a loss to the economy and should not be proceeded with for that reason.

The flaw in the thinking is that the costs being compared are not in fact comparable. The latter one is not a cost at all in the sense of the definition which will be presented later on.

The damage from the noxious emissions is a real cost because resources (wealth) are thereby depleted. Forests suffer from acid rain, through its effect on their soil. Fish and their food die off in acidified lakes. Nitrogen and sulphur oxides can add plant nourishment to topsoil up to a point, but continuous emission will eventually raise the topsoil acidity to the point where other nutrients are leached out and toxic ions such as aluminum are mobilised. Thus the topsoil resource is depleted.

The leisure and recreational value of land and water are important though less concrete economic resources. These are reduced by continuous NOx and SOx emissions. Indirect bad economic effects will follow from this because people will perceive a drop in their living standard and will tend to react as described in the chapter "Living Standard and Quality of Life."

Natural regeneration and cleansing processes that operate through soil, water, and vegetation are another important resource depleted by acid emissions.

Against all this, what is the "cost" of preventing or reducing acid emissions?

Extra resources besides the fuel must be throughput to remove the sulphur from the fuel, and/or the oxides of sulphur and nitrogen from the smoke. Extra plants must be installed and run to accomplish this. The extra resource throughput is a cost in terms of the definition presented later.

The extra plants and processes add to the price of a unit of electricity, with the following results:

Consumers use less electricity and have less to spend on other goods and services. This is described as a "cost" to the economy because of the reduced throughput.

Actually the deficiency in throughput is a gain rather than a cost. The resources that would have been put through are still there; their throughput is delayed, postponed, not irretrievably lost. The fact that less electricity, thus less fossil or nuclear fuel, is consumed and less resources are structured into goods and services as a result of lower demand, means that resources are less depleted than they would otherwise have been.

The money value of the throughput which didn't take place could be many times greater than the money value of the extra materials and processes required to clean the fuel and its combustion products. It is also apparently much greater than the money value of the damage done by acid-forming material in the fuel and its smoke. Thus the argument goes that it is better to allow the damage than to reduce the throughput.

A more thoughtful analysis would make it clear that it is nonsense to compare the loss of wealth resulting from acid emissions with the lowering of throughput, one of wealth's first derivatives. These two things being compared can somehow be expressed in cash terms, but this does not make them comparable in a simple sense of A can be expressed as more dollars than B, so throw out B to keep A.

This simple comparison is false because the monetary expression for wealth describes a quantity possessed, whereas the monetary expression for throughput describes the rate of consumption of that possession.

The fallacy is another error that stems from the wrong assumption that economic activity creates wealth; throughput is called "production" or "national income" as though it were adding to an ever-growing store of wealth. This has been discussed in other chapters.

Another example of misuse of the term "cost" is to be found in a United Nations report in which the money spent on the arms race is compared with the money supposedly required to achieve various environmental benefits. The report says that $50 billion a year are spent on the arms race, whereas safe water for all developing countries within nine years from that date would cost $7 billion, a worldwide clean air programme would cost $5 billion, and so on.

First, clean water and clean air are not costs, but gains. Two resources would have had their quantity increased. It may be that in the process other resources would be depleted, but this need not be the case. A lot of money changing hands in the process of achieving clean air and water doesn't necessarily mean that there was any cost. If the throughput rate of no other resource was raised above its renewal rate, then the whole process has been a net economic gain.

Definition of Cost

To summarise the point, and provide a basic definition of cost: when deciding whether an episode of economic activity has been a cost, and if so how much, it is no guide to measure the amount of money that changed hands. One must look at the following three criteria: (i) Has a resource been depleted? Or (ii) has the depletion rate of a resource been increased because its throughput rate now exceeds its renewal rate by a greater amount than it did before the episode of economic activity? Or (iii) is a resource being throughput now at a rate greater than its renewal rate, when before it was being renewed faster than it was being throughput? Is the resource being depleted now when it wasn't before?

Further points will be made about that UN report in the following digression.

Digression: Other Comments on Statements in UN Report

This digression makes two further comments on the statement on weapons versus other expenditure in the 1981 UN report mentioned above. One may return to this chapter later and go straight on to the chapter "Discussion of Costs Resumed," if desired.

The UN report statement also implies agreement with the conventional idea that economic activity is a process of accumulation of wealth. The achievement of clean air and water seems to be regarded as a permanent result of a particular episode of economic activity. In fact both resources are constantly throughput and their maintenance would therefore require continuous effort. This would involve any or all of the following: actively increasing the renewal rate of clean air and water, reducing interference with natural processes of renewal, and reducing the rate of throughput.

The other point is that the quantity of money exchange necessary to achieve something big like widespread clean water or air depends on (i) whether steps are in fact taken towards such achievement and (ii) what other economic activities are being started or suspended at the same time. Money itself does not bring into being clean air; this is done by the physical activity and resource throughput set in motion by the exchange of money.

At the same time, economic activities within an economic system are interdependent. The expansion or curtailment of one activity may boost or retard other activities.

A project like the securing of clean water supplies for less perfluent nations may be quite carefully estimated to require the exchange of a certain amount of money, but when the project is actually undertaken it may be affected by all sorts of constraints that greatly increase the amount of money required to change hands. This will arise from economic activity being directed in new ways that put pressure on a different set of resources in a different combination. This is not to say that the clean water will need more money than estimated; it is saying that resources being limited, it is always possible for money expense to be much higher than the estimates that were done on the basis of an assumption of unlimited resources. This assumption involves a linear relationship between effort and return in resource throughput. Resources being limited, ever more effort is required for resource throughput as the resource is depleted. The relation is nonlinear.

Discussion of Costs Resumed

Partial Accounting

Another spurious "cost" often used as a basis for policy appears as a result of partial accounting. An urban public transport service might be reduced or eliminated on the grounds that the costs of the service are nowhere near covered by passenger fares, and that costs can be reduced and the nation or city thereby enriched by cutting the service.

The error here is that all that is taken into account is the money laid out by the government on the service. This money comes from the community by way of taxes. These taxes would reduce if the service were withdrawn, but other costs to the community would increase if the buses or trains stopped running. These costs are, for example:

The increased depletion rate of fossil fuel resulting from increased use of cars.

The increased money cost of cars being run more than they otherwise would be.

Upward pressure on wages because car ownership and use has become that much more obligatory.

Downward pressure on employment, particularly at the lower skill levels, caused by the upward pressure on wages.

Increased resource consumption and money outlay associated with more frequent repair and more extensive building of roads and carparks.

A public transport service described as "uneconomic" because fare revenue falls short of money outlay is probably far more "economic" than the real alternative to running it.

A better answer to the money-losing problem of the service would be to make it more expensive in cash, and more difficult to bring private cars into high-density central business districts. This could be done by levying a large tax on petrol; restricting carparks in the high-density areas, and increasing fees for their use; giving buses priority lanes on some roads in the district and right-of-way in all parts of the district. The patronage for public transport would be boosted while fares could still be increased. The greatly increased use of public transport that would occur would reduce costs for the whole community by reducing resource depletion and private and public money outlays, relieve upward pressure on wages, and thereby save jobs.

One might argue that the increased money expense of private motoring into the high-density area would result in upward pressure on wages and downward pressure on employment. But obviously in this case people would have a choice—to use public transport instead. If public transport is eliminated, there is no choice but increased use of private cars.

Transference of Throughput

Another error related to partial accounting arises when throughput is transferred from one part of the economy to another with little or no net change in throughput, but only the throughput "debit" to one part of the economy is recorded as a so-called "cost" to the whole without taking account of the "credit" to the other part of the economy.

An example of this is the holding of an election. Much money is spent on campaigning, advertising, salaries for electoral officers, ballot papers, and so on. If as often happens in some countries, an election is called ahead of time to give the party in power some advantage, the opposition makes an issue out of the supposed "costs" of the election to the country. The entire money outlay associated with the election is described as a cost to the taxpayer. In fact all that is happening is a transfer of throughput from some economic channels to others.

The effect on total throughput is indirect and may be to increase or decrease it, according to whether the transfer worsens or alleviates any ratio distortion that may exist. During the Great Depression the holding of an election every three months might have been beneficial to economic activity.

There may be no actual cost involved in the election, in terms of extra resource depletion. Overall there may be less resource depletion. The extra resource throughput during the election will be counterbalanced by slower throughput in other areas from which throughput was transferred.

Summary

Any net depletion of resources is a cost. An episode of activity that depletes resources less than an alternative episode is less costly than the alternative.

Any reduction in throughput rate, or suspension of throughput in any part of the economy, is a gain, not a cost.

Exchange of money between one part of the economy and another is a loss of throughput to one and a gain to the other. It is not in itself a cost to the economy as a whole. It may result in an increase or decrease in the total throughput rate of the economy, depending on the effect, if any, on the relative proportions of money flowing through different economic channels. Thus the original exchange may directly lead to a cost (increased throughput of resources that either starts or accelerates their depletion) or a gain (reduced throughput) to the economy as a whole. Note the contradiction to current thinking in the last sentence.

The Problem of Government Debt

A major problem for economies around the world currently is government debt. This matter has been mentioned in other chapters. Many governments have been running a deficit on their annual budget for years. It is not universallly realised that these deficits are cumulative. A smaller deficit in the current year than in the last does not mean that government debt has fallen. Every year in which there is a deficit of any size adds to the overall government debt. At the time of writing, merely paying interest on the accumulated government debt is the third largest item in the annual budget of the U.S.A., after social security and defence, and the second largest item on Sweden's budget after social security. These payments merely take care of interest and do not reduce the principal.

Merely running reduced deficits or balanced budgets would not reduce this burden of interest payments. It would be necessary to run a surplus, year after year, and plough it straight back into reducing the principal. The effect of such a procedure, through raised taxes and reduced government spending, would be dramatic.

Three questions arise:

(i) Why did such debts pile up?
(ii) Do they matter? Do they need to be paid back?
(iii) How could they be paid back without severe economic dislocation and high unemployment?

First, the debts were incurred mainly for two reasons that have already been discussed in other chapters and will be recapitulated briefly here.

The deficit financing that helped the world out of the Great Depression was long thought to be a general remedy for any economic slowdown. In fact it was a good specific remedy for the particular type of slowdown that the Great Depression was, but for modern recessions it was necessary to go back to Keynes' theory and use it to devise different remedies. To use the Great Depression method actually aggravated the modern disease it was meant to cure and created an ever-growing public debt.

Helping this was the implicit assumption that involuntary unemployment was solely a function of the economic "growth" rate (i.e., throughput increase, TI), without any other factors affecting it. So the solution to unemployment has always been seen to be a higher TI rate and the way to achieve full employment was seen to be high TI sustained indefinitely.

Of course we have seen that endless TI is impossible and that wage levels are an important determinant of the involuntary unemployment rate.

As for private debt, the reasons for its accumulation have been discussed elsewhere.

Second, why can't the government of, for instance, the U.S.A., simply declare that the accumulated debt no longer exists, wipe the slate clean, and carry on with no red ink in the budget books?

This would be saying to all the people who put their money in the banks, individual savers, clubs, companies: "All right, all that money we've borrowed has become a free gift, thank you very much, forget about getting it back." The money borrowed by the government still belongs to all the bank's depositors; it is their property that they count among their assets and they expect to earn interest by leaving it with the bank to lend to others. For the government to announce that the federal debt no longer existed would be to grab sizable proportions of everybody's savings and profits as a totally unauthorised tax. This option is legally and politically impossible. The only reason for mentioning such an absurd idea is that far too many of the general population think it is a serious practical method of coping with deficits.

So, why can't the government simply print enough money to pay back the whole federal debt in one go? They own the mint.

Thus to increase the money supply suddenly by a large

proportion without any comparable increase in the flow of goods and services in the economy would rapidly and greatly increase the true inflation rate. This would feed on itself by reducing consumer and investor confidence, creating upward pressure on interest rates, creating an "inflationary psychology" (quite a real and powerful factor as was found in Germany in 1923), reducing economic activity, and creating upward pressure on wages. Unemployment would rise. It would be difficult to get out of the mess, having got into it. The print-more-money option is quite unthinkable. Unfortunately it has been thought of in recent history, as, for instance, Chileans know to their grief.

The answer to Question (ii) is yes, the debts do matter and there is no choice but to pay them back.

So how can this be done? Reducing debt is like losing weight. There are only two ways of losing weight; reduce food intake and increase physical activity. So with getting out of debt there are only two ways: reduce expenditure and increase income. With losing weight the difficult part is doing the two things without damaging the health of the lightening body; so with wiping off government debt, the difficult part is reducing government outlays and increasing revenue without crippling the economic system.

The difficulty here is not so much devising methods that in theory would work, but rather putting them into practice against the opposition of people to particular measures affecting them and of politicians who naturally desire to stay in office beyond the limited term between elections. The end result of getting out of debt would benefit everybody, but it is difficult to sell those long-term benefits when the price is deprivation right now.

The political problem lies beyond the scope of this chapter. If it could be made politically achievable, then the following measures are suggested.

143

Achieve sustainable full employment first by applying the wage freeze and wage indexation systems discussed in the chapters on wages and wage fixing.

Apply the reduced indexation to social security payments discussed in the chapter "Coping with Aging Populations."

Don't try to pay off the accumulated principal of the debt for a while. Keep servicing it and make the policy a firm one of not increasing it any further. This would mean achieving a balanced budget, for safety's sake one running a small surplus, for every financial year. The money amount of the principal being not increased will gradually shrink to an ever smaller fraction of total national throughput measured in money terms and of government revenue and expenditure. This will make the debt ever less threatening and easier to repay.

Budget Balancing Methods—Cost or Gain?

Measures to reduce expenditure and increase revenue raising by governments will often be seen in current economic terms as "costs" to the nation. But if seen in the light of the ideas put forward in the chapter on "Costs—What Really Costs Us and What Doesn't," they are economic gains.

Putting a tax on motor spirit will reduce the depletion rate of nonrenewable fossil fuel resources without affecting necessary transport. Motor spirit consumption everywhere, though more in some places than others, is grossly in excess of what is actually required for the transportation it provides. It is not necessary to have one to two tonnes of powerful machinery to carry one person. In concentrated business or industrial areas that could be efficiently served by mass transit it is not necessary to cram each person into the area in their own car. The point is that people could travel for work or pleasure as much as they do now using only a fraction of the liquid fuel currently used. So any tax that reduced liquid fuel consumption by raising its price would slow the rate of depletion of the resource base and thus provide a form of economic growth without reducing utility.

Yet current economics would say that (i) there would be a cost to consumers because the tax would increase their fuel bill, as though their rate of fuel consumption were an irreducible necessity—a nonsensical notion; (ii) there would be a cost to the nation because lower fuel consumption would exert downward pressure on the gross national "product." There would be so much lost "production" in the oil industry, economists would say, as though something were irrevocably lost from the ever-growing pile of national wealth that economic activity is supposed to create.

Increasing income taxes would reduce expenditure on goods and services, but this would be a gain because of the lower rate of resource depletion that would result. Paying higher income taxes would also cause people to press for higher wages, but this pressure could and should be resisted.

Income taxes could be left alone and consumption taxes introduced or increased instead. These taxes could be designed not just to raise revenue, but to reduce consumption of those resources whose consumption most needs curbing because (i) the consumption rate exceeds the renewal rate by a wide margin; (ii) the consumption of the resource is a disproportionately large part of the total resource throughput in the economy; (iii) the consumption of the resource is most in excess of the consumption actually required to provide the service obtained; (iv) the use of the resource entails the formation, with consequent leakage and disposal problems, of pollutants, substances toxic to life.

The consumption taxes could also be heavier on things

most unnecessary or dangerous to health such as cigarettes, alcohol, rich meals in expensive restaurants, or pornographic videos.

The other side, reduced government money outlays, is just as important. I reject the current fad for "privatisation." Services provided by the government are there because there is a demand for them and they are a kind that the private sector would do less well or not at all. However, gross inefficiency, measured in terms of what is actually achieved by the staff and time used, is a general disease of government bureaucracies. Far more could be achieved with the staff and time available, or the same could be achieved more quickly with fewer employees. But this is the one problem in the public sector which politicians are least able or willing to tackle. This subject will be discussed in more detail in the ensuing digression.

Digression: Government Expenditure—Government Employees

Any employee of government would be familiar with the problems peculiar to their area—the "walking dead," the top heavy hierarchy, the frequent and prolonged breaks. But it is a mistake to state sweepingly that "all civil servants are slackers." What usually happens is that a fraction of the employees do most of the work and could hold their own in the most competitive private company. A further substantial proportion do little work and are carried by their workmates. The remainder are various degrees of bosses and do little besides talk to each other, create paper, and frustrate their subordinates.

The management problem is peculiar to government service and arises in this way. It can take decades to rise to a high administrative rank during which time anyone with any talent or energy gets out to where promotion is faster and financial reward greater. The ones left behind, shuffling slowly up the promotion ladder, are the plodders, the dullards, the less qualified.

In addition, people who stay in the service for years naturally expect to get promoted, so there accumulates a thickening layer of senior officers out of proportion to the number of junior ones at the "working" level. So there are too many bosses and they lack talent.

None of the faults with government service so far mentioned are unavoidable—they are what happens by default, when things are allowed to go their own way without active intervention.

What to do about the walking dead? It is easy to say "sack 'em" but there is no one more out of work than a public servant sacked for inefficiency. A humane and practical solution must be found. If the "turkeys" are truly incapable of doing the work that their often substantial salary requires they should be retired on an invalid pension. If they are capable of the work they must be made to do it.

Every civil servant should be required to fill a quota of work performed in a given period. So one job might be assigned a maximum time for completion of say, two hours, or another might be required to be done at the rate of, say, at least one hundred per day.

Persons consistently failing to work up to the standards laid down could be put on a modified salary regime where they are paid for work performed rather than for time spent in the work place.

Conversely, people consistently doing more than their share of the work could be encouraged and rewarded by bonuses and privileges.

Promotions must be strictly determined not by the number of officers having years of dutiful service behind them, but by the number of management positions actually required for maximum efficiency. Frustration of able officers who might be tempted to leave the service to gain advancement could be relieved by industrial democracy, as follows.

All management positions should be elective and would be for a limited but not too short term, say two or three years. Only persons with some minimum period of service, say six months, would be eligible to vote, but obviously persons from outside the department or altogether outside the service would be eligible and desired to stand and would have free access to their desired place of work in order to campaign for a management position in it.

People might say this couldn't work, the service would collapse, people would get into office promising ever longer breaks and ever more indulgence of unauthorised "sickies," slack timekeeping, and nonwork activities. Presumably a parallel argument has been used in history by those opposing the development of parliamentary democracy with people electing their rulers by universal one-person-one-vote. Yet democratic countries function demonstrably better than dictatorships, whether of the proletariat or of some eccentric general.

Able people from outside the service would have to be attracted by salaries comparable with what they could command outside. This might appear to contradict the arguments elsewhere in this book against people getting salaries that allow them to consume far more than they need. This is because our present society contradicts what is necessary for a sustainable world economy. But the debt problem needs to be solved in the near future, in fact if it is not it won't be solved at all; which means it must be solved in the context of societies similar to the way they are at present, whereas the problem of people being able to consume far more than is necessary for them or desirable for the general economic welfare needs to be solved by such a radical restructuring of world society as will take a long time, being achievable only by many steps as by the mosaic method, evolution not revolution, discussed in the *Foreword.*

Having got rid of dead wood, set minimum productivity levels for everyone, reduced management to what is necessary, made people compete freely for management jobs, and made workers elect their management, one or both of two things will happen to government departments: (i) What used to be a heavy backlog and too much work will become possible to complete promptly and keep up to date using the existing staff. (ii) The reorganised department will be capable of far more work than can be foreseen for it to do. In the latter case, many staff will be redundant and some will have to be got rid of, or redeployed, straightaway without waiting for the kind processes of "attrition" by voluntary retirement or resignation of staff. This problem has struck and will continue to strike private and public organisations, and incorrect approaches are often taken to its solution.

The "first on, last off" principle might seem fair but some of the "last on" might be in more desperate need of a job and might find it more difficult to get another than many who have worked longer with the place. It is not a crime to have started working somewhere later than someone else and people should not have to suffer a penalty on that account. Also, some later starters might have special individual skills or they might occupy positions which are harder to fill.

Traditionally, if circumstances have arisen necessitating large numbers of sackings, it is the women who have been pushed out first. The arguments have been "They're married and ought to be at home being supported by and caring for their husbands and producing children to make the nation richer and stronger" or "They ought to be married and have a man to support them" or "They're just filling in time till

149

they get married" or "They can always work in a brothel making a good living exploiting us poor men" or "Their hormones make them unreliable and they talk all day instead of working."

This injustice against women must have no place in the future. In many countries legal institutions are being created that hope to end discrimination against women, but there is still a long way to go. Discrimination is still possible in myriad subtle ways that are harder for the law to reach. Women must generally be more aware, take more interest, and make more noise against injustice. There are plenty of sympathetic males who would help, but the women must take the initiative.

A fairer system than hitherto of deciding who would be dismissed might score the employee according to the following criteria, not necessarily in this order:

How many dependents has the person? Can any of them become financially independent and how long will this take?

What are this person's chances of getting another job?

How important is this person, not just in the position they occupy but in their personal qualities, to this place?

How long has the person been here (this criterion is all right to use in combination with others)?

How long was the person out of work before starting with us?

What are the person's financial circumstances?

These criteria should be weighted according to importance and computed to a total score. If a hundred sackings were required, the hundred employees with the lowest scores would be given notice. It would be necessary to be quite firm about this, otherwise it could drag on and lose some of its cost-effectiveness.

The Role of Religion

The Christian religion displays a paradox. It claims to be about love and life, while containing in all its denominations and offshoots (particularly Shi'ite Islam) many strong manifestations of death-orientation or necrophilia.

I use the term necrophilia in its broadest sense, which I will define thus: the passionate attraction to all that is dead, decayed, putrid, sickly; the passion to transform something alive into something unalive, and to destroy for the sake of destruction; the exclusive interest in all that is purely mechanical or inanimate; the passion to tear apart living structures; the hatred of life, its growth and development and its sources.

Necrophilia shows itself in many forms, some relatively benign and passive, some more active and dangerous. Any form can transmute into any other depending on the circumstances and on opportunities presented.

Examples follow of necrophilous manifestations in Christianity. After these it will be suggested how the paradox might be resolved.

The central prominent symbol of Christianity is the same as the death symbol—the cross. It represents death, in the shape of the means of execution in ancient Rome. Often a model corpse is nailed to the cross.

A tendency towards dark clothing, plain designs, sombre shades, gloomy interiors. Such things have traditionally seemed more proper to Christianity than light, colour, and beauty. During the Protestant reformation, the aspects of Catholicism rejected by the reformers in trying to get back to true Christianity included most of the ornamental, artistic side of it. Bright vestments, elaborate ornament, great music were discarded as improper, "Popish Trumperies." Martin Luther spoke and wrote in strongly scatological terms. It is regarded as more Christian to walk a grey path through life, to deny sensual pleasure and beauty and gratification, to regard this life as a wretched interval, and to look forward to the "hereafter" the "afterlife," ostensibly meaning a better life in a perfect place not on earth, but in reality meaning death.

Laughter and fun and sensual delight are at best regarded as slightly naughty, tolerable only under restriction, treated as a lapse from the proper mode of behaviour. Solemnity is virtue.

St Augustine of Hippo was an adherent of Manichaeism before his conversion to Christianity. The Manichaeist philosophy taught that existence was a conflict between the powers of darkness and the powers of light. Flesh and all fleshly things were identified as evil and one had to deny, mortify, and eventually shed the living body and everything to do with it in order to cleave towards the powers of light.

This is a necrophilous doctrine. Why did Augustine find it so easy to become a Christian after years of dedication to this doctrine? Why did he never abandon Manichaeism? Rather he continued to promote it. Why did it work its way so comfortably into Christianity at that time? Why was Augustine made a bishop and eventually canonised? It is true that Manichaeism was always condemned as a heresy by the church and finally stamped out, but history is full of conflicts between doctrines where doctrine A sucks the substance from doctrine B and stamps on the shell. Also, destructive rivalry tends to be stronger between doctrines when they are most similar rather than when they are most different.

The Roman Empire became ever more intensely necrophilous with age. Yet it was in its last stages that Christianity took hold. There was never great wrenching conflict between the new, supposedly life-loving philosophy and the imploding cesspit culture. Was it because Rome was too weak to resist, or was it because the new religion, despite its outward claims, was fundamentally a natural graft onto the culture?

Christianity and sex have never got along. Societies in which Christianity is or has been dominant may be becoming ever more secular, but they reflect the attitudes to sex that spring from Christianity. Even the extreme forms of permissiveness visible recently, and the sex industry of brothels, strip shows, and dirty books and videos are consistent with the traditional restrictiveness in the sense that they degrade sex and women where the old restrictions denied and suppressed sex and women.

It is regarded as best never to have had sex at all. The mother of Christ was supposed never to have had it. This is the Christian ideal. She is described as immaculate, without spot of sin. Virginity is also called virtue or chastity. The clear implication of the use of these words is that sex is dirty, evil. The fact that it is the very fount of life and expression of love doesn't seem to redeem it. Perhaps these qualities are its main faults in Christian eyes?

In Christian societies the words "virgin" and "maiden" are used generally to mean unspoilt, untouched, in the best state, as though the loss of virginity always meant defilement and degradation.

Giving up sex has always been necessary to advance in religious life, as though God represented the opposite to the life-and-love force of sex.

Killing is permissible for Christians, even desirable in a "just war" or to "defend the country against enemies, especially atheistic ones" (actual quote from an Australian catholic priest). War, even annihilating nuclear war, is regarded as preferable to atheistic communism. Surely even North Korea is better off under communism than it would be after a nuclear war? The Spanish Inquisition is still a byword for atrocious tortures and disgusting executions. Many other examples could be found.

Violence was spread across the large and small screen for decades, while it was not permitted to show a man and woman in bed together. Often children were allowed to see a war film as long as it didn't contain any kissing scenes. Only today with sexually explicit scenes on the screen are Christians trying to get TV and films cleaned up. It's true that "sex and violence" are ostensibly the targets, but when there was only violence, there was no cleanup campaign.

It is seen as quite all right to festoon Christian churches with guns and swords for ornament. It sounds insane to suggest that instead they should be decorated with pictures of naked women, babies, lovers. But why?

Another manifestation of necrophilia is the bias of Christians towards "free enterprise" as an economic and political system. This system is very necrophilous, as the following show:

(i) It presents the endless accumulation of inanimate material goods and money as the prime aim of individuals and society.

(ii) It progressively decreases the life-sustaining capacity of the environment, converting living structures to lifeless chaos at an ever-increasing rate (communism does this too, but less efficiently).

(iii) In its adherence to the principle of consuming as much as you can today, ignoring tomorrow, it denies the concern for the future that is a mark of biophilia, life-lovingness, expressed in the urge to have children.

(iv) Free enterprise degrades the role of sex as the fount of life and gives primacy to a role for it as a pleasant sensation to be used as an advertising tool; in effect to serve inanimateness, lifelessness, rather than life.

Living things evolve over time to become better-adapted, more advanced life-forms, for example, the evolution of apes into human beings. Evolution is intrinsic to life. It is denied by fundamentalist Christianity, according to which all life-forms were created at a definite time and remain the same forever. This is a necrophilous, life-hating view in that it imposes on living things qualities more suited to dead or inanimate things.

The ceremony of holy communion, in which bread and wine representing God's body and blood are eaten to give divine grace to the eater, is strongly necrophilous.

Christians tend to take the strongest "right wing"and necrophilous stands on issues: in favour of nuclear weapons buildup, against gun control, anti-environmentalism, against social welfare spending, tolerant or supportive of racism, materialism, militarism. They are also those who take the strongest stand against abortion. This appears to be a life-loving concern, but consider the following.

Necrophilia is evident in the greater care of practitioners of religion for people after death than during life. Much prayer and elaborate funerals and obituaries are often devoted to people who, while alive, were allowed to cough and starve in neglect and loneliness. It could be said that the concern for people before birth, even at the moment of conception, is motivated by necrophilia, analogous to the concern for them after death, at the expense of the living person in between. Also an abortion is often the only way to save the mother's life and health.

Of course many antiabortionists are motivated by the sincere belief that killing unborn children is murder and therefore not an acceptable solution to the problems that drive women to seek abortions.

How can this paradox of a religion that claims to be about life while being riddled with necrophilia be resolved?

We could assume that Christianity is fundamentally good and that evil men have turned it to evil purposes and tainted it with evil. Or that love of life is the founding principle of Christianity and that the elements of necrophilia are alien to it, introduced by people who wished to turn it to the service of death and of inanimate things.

But what if we turn these assumptions on their heads?

Assume that religion is fundamentally evil and that the good in it has been put there by good people trying to turn it to good purposes? The singer, not the song?

Assume that necrophilia is the founding principle, the essential nature, of religion, and that any life love is alien to it, put there by lovers of life (including Christ himself) who wished it to be a vehicle for their love?

If this were true, how could it be explained?

Human beings, alone among creatures, are aware of their inevitable death, and the intelligence that brings this awareness brings fear of death. The complete dissolution into black nothingness of everything one knows and loves is fearful and hard to accept. But it won't go away. How to deal with it?

One way is by cloaking the unacceptable face of death in a mask that makes it acceptable, even lovely. No longer an enemy that waits to tip us into nothingness, death becomes a beautiful friend who waits to take us into a new life, not only infinitely better than this one, but eternal, no end, no death.

On our fear of death and its working out through necrophilia the whole structure of religion is built.

God and the Devil are both anthropomorphisms for the same thing—death. God represents the false face of death, a beautiful loving friend. The Devil, Satan, represents the true face of death that we must shun, hate, and fear.

So, necrophilia is the black heart of religion. It keeps popping through in various form in every aspect of religion. It taints everything it touches.

If we look again at religion on this basis, everything falls into place.

Christ himself was an anomaly; he tried to make the

Jewish religion into a force for life love. But after he was gone it reverted to the same old thing, though with different outward forms. Christ remains trapped like a fly in amber, as a corpse nailed to a cross or to be eaten symbolically; identified with God, ever present in the hearts of the "saved" as a friend, more important than any of the living people around them and eliminating the other great human fear, that of being alone.

Religion is a phase in human development through which we must pass, not an essential or permanent part of human nature. We have to find some other way of coming to terms with the reality and inevitability of death. We have to exchange one paradox for another. We have to escape from the paradox of being alive, but death loving; and embrace the paradox of loving life while understanding that we all must die.

That final paradox is resolved when we realise that though we die as individuals, the human race lives on, and our life after death takes place through our children and through our creative efforts during life.

It follows from this chapter that people concerned for the conservation and enhancement of life on earth must oppose and strive to eliminate religion, particularly Judeo-Christian and Islamic forms.

Expenditure on Weapons

Huge sums are spent by governments on weapons and troops, particularly in certain countries. There are two remedies for this drain on government expenditure, one long-term and one short-term. The long-term answer lies in the evolution of the world human community towards political and economic unity—that is unity in the cooperative rather than in the monolithic sense. As this evolution proceeds, the need for large armed forces with massive sophisticated expensive weapons systems will diminish, along with the need for expenditure on them.

The short-term answer is that even if one grants a temporary need for huge armies and costly weapons, money is spent on them in a grossly inefficient way. This scandal has been well documented in the case of the U.S.A. Hundreds of dollars are sometimes paid for one small item such as a hex nut or screwdriver. Huge sums are spent on items that have nothing to do with the nation's defence and ought to come out of the private expenditure of service people or industry employees. Weapons systems cost many times more than projected and don't work, or function unreliably, at the end of it. Redundant or obsolete weapons systems gain continued funding because the industries that they support are in some politician's district or because powerful interests have their noses in the trough.

The solution to this problem of inefficient expenditure is political and moral and lies beyond the scope of this book.

Conclusion

It has not been the aim of this book to provide detailed remedies for every current problem in or related to economics. It has only been my purpose to outline a more practical and realistic relationship between the human economy and the world we live in, one which favours life over death, progress and enhancement over degeneration. If the ideas in this book be sound, then others can develop and build upon them in the future to quicken our step towards a sustainable, peaceful human world.